because I said I would.

ALEX SHEEN

GREENLEAF
BOOK GROUP PRESS

Published by Greenleaf Book Group Press
Austin, Texas
www.gbgpress.com

Distributed by Greenleaf Book Group

For ordering information or special discounts for bulk purchases, please contact Greenleaf Book Group at PO Box 91869, Austin, TX 78709, 512.891.6100.
For more information about because I said I would's charitable programs, speaking engagements, or fundraising, please visit becauseIsaidIwould.com

Design and composition by Greenleaf Book Group
Cover design by Greenleaf Book Group
Photo of Brad Corbett Sr. by Linda Kaye, courtesy of Eric Nadel

Cataloging-in-Publication data is available.

Print ISBN: 978-1-62634-534-8

eBook ISBN: 978-1-62634-535-5

Part of the Tree Neutral® program, which offsets the number of trees consumed in the production and printing of this book by taking proactive steps, such as planting trees in direct proportion to the number of trees used: www.treeneutral.com

Printed in the United States of America on acid-free paper

19 20 21 21 22 23 24   11 10 9 8 7 6 5 4 3

First Edition

Dad,

Greg and I miss you so much. We think about
you a lot. Your boys will always love you.

Contents

because I said I would.

The Beginning

....

Early one morning in the '90s, my dad was sitting quietly at the kitchen table, slowly drinking his coffee and smoking his morning cigarette. At about six years old, I was almost comically the opposite. I was running around the house in a way that was annoying to anyone old enough to understand the word *mortgage*.

Suddenly, my dad yelled at me in a stern voice. "Alex, get over here!"

I could tell he was using his "angry voice" that only a genuine dad can possess.

Not knowing what I had done, I timidly walked over to the kitchen table and stared up at him.

"Yes, Dad?" I asked.

"Alex," he said, "your room is too messy. I buy you all these toys and games, and you leave them all over the floor. You need to go up to your room and clean it right now. But here's the deal. You clean your room, and I will give you fifty cents. Okay?"

I looked at my father.

I didn't say anything.

I turned around and scrambled up the stairs. I ran down the hallway and into my bedroom, which was right above the kitchen, where my father was sitting. Through the ceiling, he could hear my little feet moving across the floor, pushing things around my room. Then, in a unit of time that was obviously not long enough to do any real cleaning, I ran back down the stairs to where my dad was sitting.

I looked him in the eye, threw two quarters on the kitchen table, and said, "You do it."

He probably didn't think it was funny in the moment, but as time passed, this would become Dad's favorite story about me. He used to tell the story just like that, except with a Chinese accent.

In 1974, at seventeen, my father moved to the United States from Hong Kong. His first name was Wei Min, but everyone just called him Al. I must have heard too many immigrant jokes as a kid because for the majority of my life I thought my father came to America on a boat. Nope. He definitely came on a commercial airplane. After all, it was 1974, not 1874.

Dad started out somewhere in Michigan, but he eventually put down roots in Ohio, where he met my mom, Angela, and where my brother and I have always called home. My brother, Greg, was born in 1983, and I came along to annoy him in 1985. While we were still very young, Dad worked as a short-order breakfast cook and a waiter at a couple of different restaurants while he went to college for pharmacy. He eventually earned his degree, went on to get his MBA, and became a successful pharmacist, working in the same hospital system for twenty-five years.

Probably the most stereotypical thing about my dad was that

he was an extremely hardworking immigrant. Dad understood what it meant to be poor and feared that he would end up that way again. I remember him telling me a story that took place not too long after he moved to America. He was living in a house with about six other people. Many of them worked at the same restaurant he did. Dad told me about how hard it was to make a living back then. One day, my father was down to his very last twenty-six cents. He remembered the exact amount. He stared at those coins in his hand, and he cried. That day, he promised himself that he would never allow himself to be that poor again. And because of hard work, he never was.

Even when it wasn't necessary, my dad would often work two jobs. I remember him working a full week at the hospital and then taking a part-time job at a retail pharmacy located hours out of town, so he could work the weekends too. He did this when he was in his fifties. Dad was determined to retire early, and he understood what he needed to do to make that happen.

My dad's work ethic had at least one

Me (left) and my brother, Greg (right)

positive effect on his role as a father. He was good at keeping the promises he made to me and my brother. My dad was far from a perfect person, but if he said he was going to be there, he showed up. If Dad said he was going to be at one of my middle school lacrosse games, I didn't look into the stands wondering if he was going to make it—I only looked to see where he was sitting. If he said he was going to pay for my college education, the check was already in the mail. My dad didn't care that promises were hard to keep. *If you say it, you do it.*

As a child, and even in my twenties, I thought this type of determination and commitment must have skipped a generation. By my father's standards, I must have been born lazy—an inheritance he thought could only come from my mother. The story of the two quarters on the kitchen table illustrates his point.

Fast-forward to 2011. My father is fifty-four years old and perhaps sitting at that same kitchen table when his cell phone rings. He turns it over and sees that it's the hospital calling. This is where my father works, so he has to answer. Dad swipes the screen to take the call. On the other line is a friend of his, a doctor who works at the hospital. They start talking, and my father soon realizes that this call is not about work. It's about a lab test that Dad has taken recently after having a bout of pneumonia.

In this phone conversation, my father was informed that he had been diagnosed with stage IV small-cell lung cancer.

My father started smoking cigarettes when he was a teenager. After decades of the habit, he quit smoking three years before he was diagnosed. Unfortunately, the cancer had already taken its hold. But my father was a "go down swinging" kind of man. He came to this country as an immigrant and he knew what it was like to struggle to survive. He wasn't about to leave without a fight.

With this attitude, my dad elected for the most aggressive treatments. He started radiation and chemotherapy.

A lot of people are familiar with the word *chemotherapy*, but few know what it actually is. Chemotherapy is literally a poison. Developed prior to World War II, chemotherapy is based on a primitive concept. The idea is to poison the body so deeply that the cancer cannot survive—but maybe that's the only way to give the patient a chance. As a pharmacist in a hospital system for twenty-five years, my father knew more about the drugs he was taking than a lot of people ever will, and with that knowledge comes a distinct

understanding of the odds that are against you. In the case of my father, those odds were terrible. But if you work in a hospital long enough, you will see people who do beat the odds. My dad believed he could be one of them.

The tumor was so close to my father's heart that it was surgically inoperable. Fortunately, with chemo and radiation, the tumor actually began to shrink. Over time, it shrunk so small that you couldn't see it on any of the numerous medical scans they did on my dad. Even he—the most genuine of skeptics, I assure you—deemed it some sort of miracle that perhaps he was saved.

Me and my dad

I will never be able to find the words to accurately describe the sense of relief that overcame me. That relief quickly turned into a burning need to celebrate victory. My dad paid for me to go to college, so I was pretty good at celebrating at this point. I went to my father and said, "This is amazing news, Dad! Okay, listen, old man. We've got to celebrate! *Anywhere* you want go! *Anything* you want to do! *Money is no object.* Okay, Dad, let's hear it. Where do you want to go? What do you want to do?"

Waiting in anticipation, I thought he was going to say something exciting, like the Bahamas, New Zealand, or Disneyland.

Nope.

"I want Chinese food."

Dad wanted to go to a Chinese restaurant we'd been to seven trillion times. He was boring like that. But you know how dads are—they have a routine, and they like what they like. I was hoping for something more ridiculous, but it was his day, so he got to choose. You can't argue with that. We had a great time eating at a Chinese restaurant that one of his buddies owned. It was a great night.

You have no idea what I would do for the chance to live that night again. I would give you a *fortune* for just five more minutes. But cancer doesn't care how much you love your father. In less than a year, the cancer would return to my father's lungs. It would spread to his liver, to his pancreas, and to his brain.

On September 4, 2012, the sun shined through the curtains of my father's house. I visualize that morning more than I would like to. I went to my father's bedside with my brother and my stepmom. I played some music for my father that I thought he might like. I held his hand, and, with the best of my ability as his son, I desperately tried to comfort him. I told him not to worry about his boys. I told him that he raised us well and that we were going to be okay. Then I told him to let go. At 11:31 a.m., I said goodbye to my dad for the last time.

Before the funeral, I was asked by my family to give my father's eulogy, to speak of his greatest quality as a man. I kept coming back to this thought: *the importance of a promise.* Too often in life, people say things like, "I'll get to it," or, "Tomorrow." But one day, there is no tomorrow. The promises that we make and keep *and* those we choose to dishonor—they are what define us. They define our character. They always have. It was that way long before my father was ever born, and it will be that way long after I die. Perhaps the greatest measure of honor is how we treat our promises.

I gave my father's eulogy and titled the speech "because I said I would." I talked about the importance of a promise that day at his funeral. And, for the very first time, I handed out what I would call *Promise Cards.* On the front, the cards say *because I said I would.* On the back, there is nothing.

The Promise Card is a simple concept. You write a promise on the card. Maybe it's something small you said today, or maybe it's something so deep that it defines part of your purpose for being on this planet. You give that card to the person that you're making that promise to, and you tell them, "I'm going to fulfill this promise, and when I do, I will earn that card back. This card is a symbol of my honor. It is my property, and I'm coming back for it." You fulfill your promise, you earn your card back, and you keep it as a reminder that you are a person of your word—maybe someone like Al Sheen was to his sons.

When my father's funeral ended, I went home. The next thing I did set off a chain of events, the scope of which I may never understand. This is where the Internet enters the story. I made a post online. It was an offer. I said that I would mail ten Promise Cards to *anyone, anywhere* in the world at *no cost* to *anybody*.

That gesture became two important and life-changing things:

1. The start of a social movement around the world

2. The dumbest financial decision I have ever made

Because I said I would has
distributed more than

10.3

million

Promise Cards to more than 157 countries, by request only.

Kids, don't offer free stuff to strangers on the Internet. You see, getting five requests for Promise Cards in a day is no big deal. You wake up early, pack a few envelopes, feed your dog, laugh at a few memes as you brush your teeth, pack a few more envelopes, and so on—a few here and there. That's how life feels at five requests in a day. But what if you were to get 50 requests overnight? Then all of a sudden, the number is 500. Now think about 15,000 requests in a single day. What do you do when it goes viral? I had to figure that out.

I learned about the importance of a promise not just from my father, but from humanity itself. People around the world started posting pictures of their Promise Cards and the stories behind them on social media. Complete strangers would find inspiration in those messages, and they would ask *because I said I would* for cards to make their own promises. Pictures of those cards were posted, and the loop would start again.

This book is an attempt to describe what happened when I accidentally started a chain reaction. It's about the impact that promises have on the world and the life lessons they teach.

Because I said I would is a social movement and nonprofit dedicated to the betterment of humanity through promises made and kept. It started as a eulogy to my father, but it has grown into a force far greater than its origin.

I must insist that this is not a business book. In fact, if someone bought you this book trying to motivate you for commercial purposes, please return it to them and point to this sentence. Yes, promises connect with all parts of life, but we are a humanitarian effort and nothing else. I hope that becomes plain to see in the pages to come.

I must also warn you that this book is not in chronological order, nor is it separated into well-defined themes. There are seven sections about our Code of Honor, but those don't create clean division between principles or character values. The somewhat random nature of this book presents the same challenge that was presented to me. Stories just flooded in and realizations did not always come to me in a neat package. The meaning of each promise story wasn't always immediately clear. Sometimes, I got to know supporters on a personal level, and other times, the promise was only an image shared on social media with no context. Somehow, the stories built meaning on one another all by them-

selves. As the thousands on thousands of messages poured in, it took time for the bigger picture to show itself.

I need to apologize in advance to my longtime supporters expecting extended accounts of my personal promises. While this book is certainly written from my perspective, I made a very intentional decision not to include many of my personal promises and only lightly cover the handful of ones I do talk about. This movement was never intended to be about me; I was just trying to do my part and lead by example. Trust me, though—our supporters' promise stories are much stronger and more insightful than my commitments can ever be.

Please know that, to my knowledge, this is a book of true

stories. While it is possible that I have made some unintentional errors, I interviewed our supporters and have tried to describe their stories as accurately as reasonable based on their accounts.

Our supporters gave me hope when I needed it the most. I just hope I can do their stories justice. ■

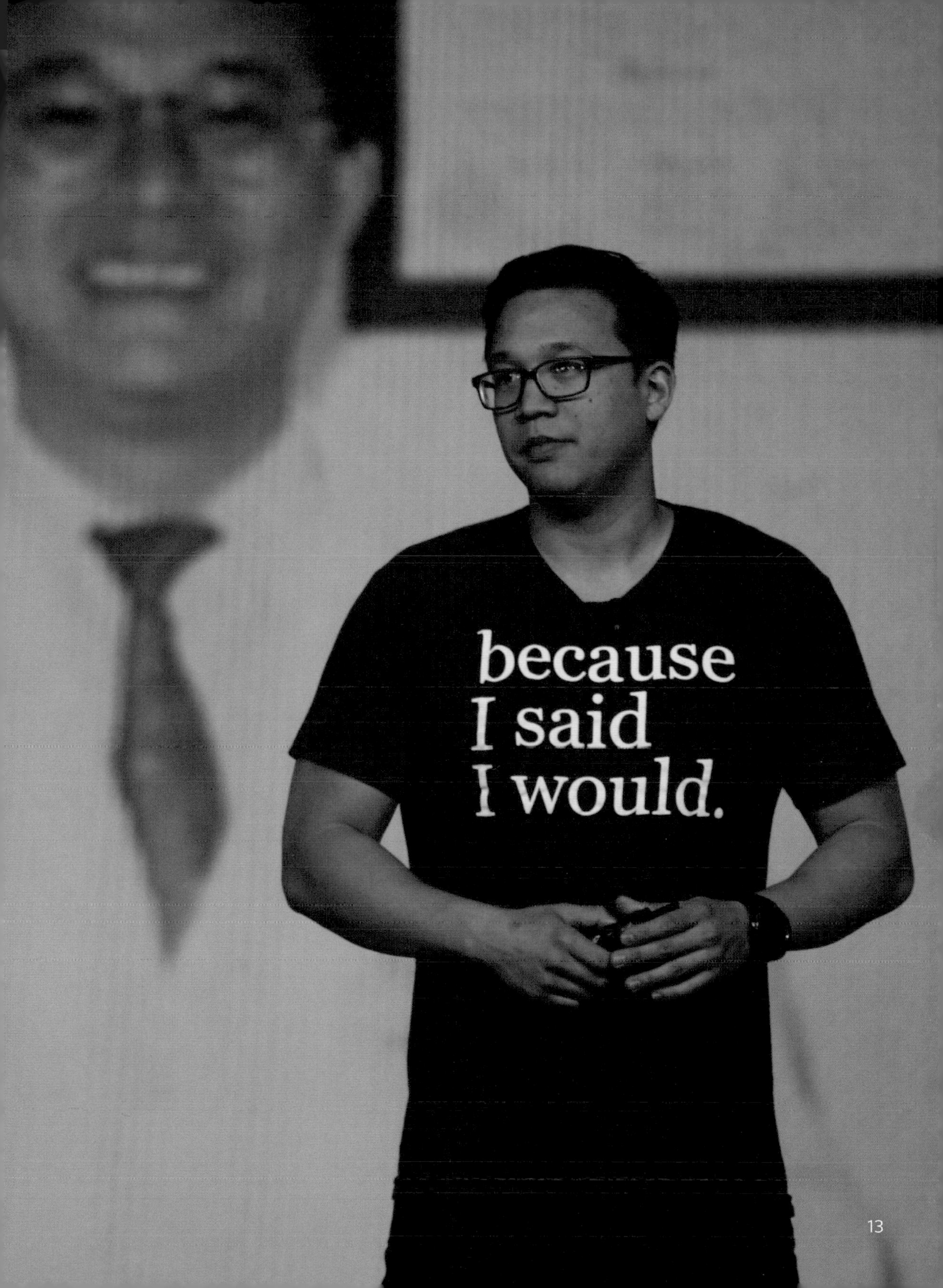
because
I said
I would.

because I said I would.

I promise to finally break free from my abusive husband.

because I said I would.

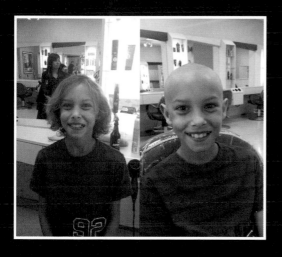

◀ "AT FIRST, PEOPLE ASKED ME, 'Do you have cancer?'

"I said, 'No, I actually just donated.' At the beginning, it was good because I was in elementary school and everyone is nice and kind. But when I got into middle school and I did it again, some kids started making fun of me. But I realized that I'm doing something good. It doesn't matter what they think."

Benjamin Awad's family uses Promise Cards as a reminder of what's important in life. He carries a pack in his book bag.

I will honor the gift of my sister's kidney every moment I am alive ...

because I said I would.

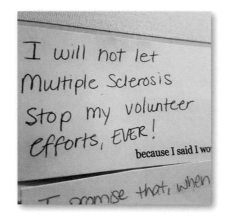

I will show my neighbor kindness even though he hates me because of my race and religion.

because I said I would.

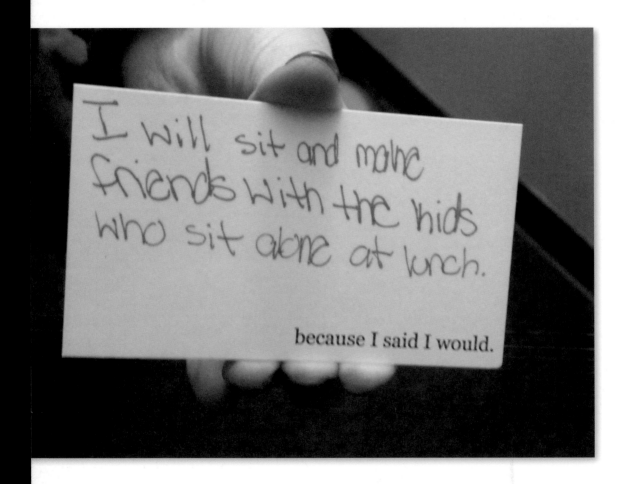

Anonymous

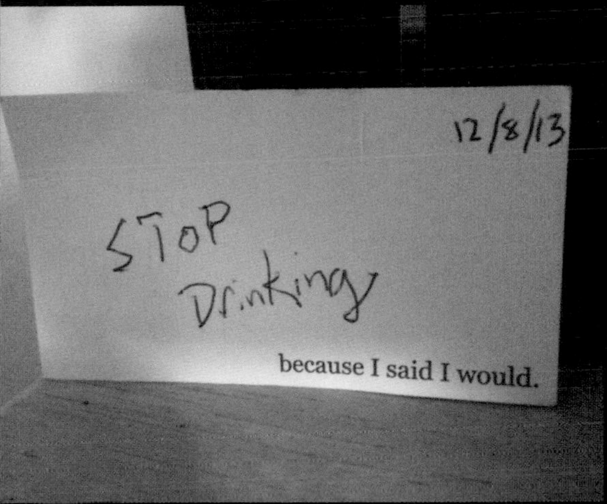

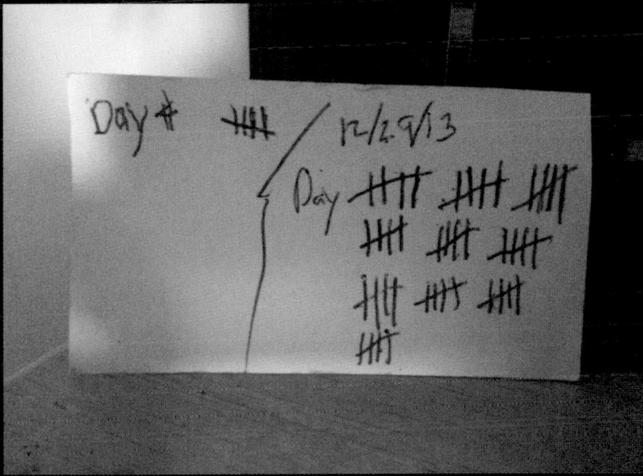

Fail.
Try again.
Fail.
Try again.

The Son of a Firefighter

Apples Come from Apple Trees

Bobby O'Donnell grew up in a town called Easton, about twenty minutes outside of Boston. As a kid, his greatest hero *and* his greatest source of embarrassment was his dad. Bob Senior had a very dad-like sense of humor that made his son cringe, as sons will do. But that sense of humor helped counterbalance the seriousness of Bob Senior's job. He is a fire department shift commander.

In elementary school, it is an epic occasion when the fire department comes to the school for a fire drill. The trucks are massive. The gear is heavy. Imagine growing up as the son of a firefighter. One of those people is *your dad*. It is something to be proud of.

A lot of Bobby's life has been influenced by his dad's profession. When Bobby turned sixteen in 2010, his dad taught him how to drive in the parking lot of the firehouse. But because Bob Senior's profession focused on safety, it wasn't your typical experience. Bob Senior set up traffic cones about twenty-five feet apart, and Bobby had to swerve the car between the cones at a moderate speed. Like something out of an '80s movie training montage, his father would simulate a ninja-style deer ambush by hurling cones in front of the car as Bobby was driving.

Maybe it was because Bobby grew up around heroes in uniform, but in high school, a very particular goal formed in Bobby's mind. Around the Boston area, there is a distinctive jacket that Bostonians can easily spot from a block away. This is not a jacket you can simply buy; you have to earn it. It is the official jacket for the Boston Marathon, the world's oldest annual marathon and one of the best-known racing events ever held. When you're a seventeen-year-old runner in high school, that jacket represents a kind of determination that you want to have—maybe something like a firefighter's jacket.

However, there are only two ways to get into the Boston Marathon: One is to be a really, really fast runner. The second is to raise over $5,000 for the Boston Children's Hospital. Bobby was a typical American kid in many ways, including his running pace, so speed wasn't going to be his way in. Instead, Bobby turned his sights to fundraising and began volunteering at the children's hospital. After witnessing firsthand the disease and injury those kids had to go through, suddenly the jacket didn't seem so important. As Bobby puts it, "It meant so much to me to be able to run for people other than myself, to have people counting on me. It wasn't just my race anymore."

In 2013, Bobby O'Donnell was twenty years old and signed up to run the Boston Marathon for the first time. His whole family was excited for this challenge—so much so that Bobby's dad and other family members accompanied him to pick up his race bib (i.e., his runner identification number) the day before the race. Because of the massive scale of this marathon, runners collect their bibs at a gigantic trade expo packed with health-related vendors representing everything from shoes to protein cookies. As the O'Donnells walked through this convention center, Bob Senior's attention was captured by a booth selling very high-end Japanese massage chairs.

"Oh Bobby, you've got to try that chair. It's gonna be great for your run!"

"Dad, I'm not gonna do that."

"C'mon! Really? Well, you know what? I'll try it."

As his dad climbed into the chair, Bobby saw a little smirk develop on his father's face, a smirk that is all too familiar to Bobby. It's the face a father has when he is about to do something he thinks is funny.

Bob Senior taking a picture at the runner's trade expo wearing his son's racing bib.

As Bob Senior settled into the massage chair and pressed the *on* button, he closed his eyes and let out a little sound. "Oooo."

It was just loud enough that the people around him could hear it. Seeing where this was going, Bobby started slowly backing away. Disassociation was his plan.

"Oh yeaaaah . . ." said Bob Senior, this time more loudly, eyes still closed as the massage chair picked up momentum. His declarations of pleasure grew in volume. His facial expressions were cartoonish. *"That's the spot!"*

A crowd started to gather. It became a scene. People couldn't help but look. Some were staring; others were laughing. Cell phones were pulled from pockets and purses. People began recording a mustached, middle-aged man moaning in delight.

After what seemed like an eternity to his son, the massage chair slowed to a stop. Bob Senior then hoisted himself from the chair, looked the salesman directly in the eye, and delivered his punch line: "I'll take it!"

The crowd applauded. Bobby buried his face in his hands, but he laughed as well. Bob Senior wanted to give the chair salesman a boost with this whole show he put on, but he also put his money where his mouth was: Bob Senior paid for the chair (which cost over $4,000). He asked very carefully about the return policy: ninety days money back. After the transaction, the O'Donnells went on their way, collecting Bobby's race bib before heading home.

When the day of the Boston Marathon finally arrived, Bobby was ready to leave the house at 5:00 a.m. In the darkness of the morning, Bobby and his dad got into the family's old Toyota Avalon, which had over 300,000 miles on the odometer. Bob Senior drove Bobby to the shuttle pickup point for the race.

As the sun started to rise over the city, Bob Senior turned to his son and said, with no humor in his voice, "Bobby, I can't tell you how proud I am of you. I don't think you realize how many lives you've touched by doing this. You did all the hard work. Now it's race day. Just go enjoy the race." He gave his son a big hug, and then Bobby climbed out of the car and watched his dad drive away. That's the first time it all felt real to Bobby. The time had come. At around 11:00 in the morning, Bobby O'Donnell started running the Boston Marathon.

It might sound strange, but for many people, the start of a marathon actually feels like a type of finish line in itself. You're finished with training. You're finished with fundraising. The race can feel like a victory lap. There are mental milestones along the way. At mile one, you remember a donor. At mile two, maybe you remember a child in the hospital. Another mile done and perhaps you flashback to an early morning when nothing in you wanted to get up to train, but you did it anyway. As Bobby ran mile after mile, making his way east along flats and over rolling hills toward the heart of the city, he acknowledged each of these milestones in his mind.

Anyone who has run the Boston Marathon likely knows the unique phrase "Right on Hereford, left on Boylston." At the very end of the race, there are two quick turns on these streets before you reach the finish line. You are physically close to the end, but because of all the buildings, you can't see it yet. After hours of running, Bobby could see Hereford Street when he heard a crashing sound. Then another. But cities are loud places. This was downtown Boston. It would be weird if there *weren't* any loud noises, so no one around Bobby thought anything of it.

But then police officers began to filter their way into the running path of the race. They said to the runners, "Hold up here for now." For many runners, this marathon is a once-in-a-lifetime moment. Stopping didn't make sense, even if an officer was telling you to, so many of the runners bypassed the police, ignored their words, and kept going.

Maybe it's because of his particular respect for law enforcement and public service, but Bobby listened and stopped running. Nevertheless, he was still puzzled over why anyone would stop the Boston Marathon.

Bobby jogged in place, trying to stay warm. No one could tell him what was going on.

Minutes later, Bobby saw something surreal. People were running *away* from the finish line. He asked one of those people, "What's going on?"

Bobby will never forget the crazed look on this woman's face. She told him that there were two explosions at the finish line of the Boston Marathon. "They blew up the grandstands," she told him.

Bobby's heart felt like it had stopped beating. His family came to support him that day, and they got tickets to sit in the grandstands to watch him finish. Bobby didn't have a cell phone; he never ran with one. (He does now.) He stopped a passing news reporter and borrowed a cell phone. One by one, he called his mom's number and his dad's and his grandmother's. Each time he called, it was the same response.

"This number is out of service and cannot be reached."
"This number is out of service and cannot be reached."
"This number is out of service and cannot be reached."

As he handed the cell phone back to the reporter, what was happening started to sink in. Bobby believed that his whole family had been killed.

He walked on in a daze. The finish line area was blocked off, and he couldn't get anywhere near it. He sat on a stoop for a while and then asked another stranger if he could borrow her phone to try just one more time. This time he texted his mom instead of calling her.

I'm okay. Are you okay? he wrote.

His mom replied almost immediately. *Who is this?*

In the rush, Bobby had forgotten to say who he was. *This is Bobby. I'm texting from a borrowed phone. I'm okay. Where are you?*

The woman who told Bobby the bombs went off in the grandstands was misinformed. Those bombs exploded across from the grandstands. Bobby's family was safe.

His mom texted him back. *Meet me at Fenway Park.*

Bobby immediately ran to Fenway and found his family. In tears, he embraced his mom, grandmother, aunt, and cousin. He was so relieved to see them, but then he noticed that his dad wasn't there.

As the bombs exploded across from the grandstands, Bob Senior directed his family and others to safety. Then he headed in the direction a firefighter goes—toward the danger.

Bob Senior jumped over a barrier, across the path of the race, and into the other side of the street, where the explosion occurred. Perhaps it's human nature to want to stop and help the first person who is screaming in pain, but Bob Senior was trained to fight that instinct. His priority was to first help those who were most critically injured and closest to death. To do that, he needed to find the center of the explosion. Injuries are naturally most fatal at this point and become less severe as you move farther out. It is a cold thought but a necessary one: *Don't stop until you have found a dead body.*

In the midst of the chaos, he came to a woman who was lying on the pavement, completely still. She was already gone. He had no choice but to move on. Bob Senior then found a man lying in a pool of blood. Both of his legs had been blown off. "I had never seen someone with such catastrophic injuries that was still alive," Bob remembers. Using a piece of cloth, he applied a tourniquet to one of his legs. He knew this man was in bad shape. That man was Jeff Bauman, who became one of the most recognized survivors of the bombing.

Bob Senior continued to help where he could, directing people to apply tourniquets, put pressure on glass-inflicted wounds, and help get casualties in ambulances. With thirty-five years of experience as a firefighter and an overlapping thirty-nine years of experience as an emergency room nurse, Bob Senior was in the wrong place at the right time. "He just tried to do anything he could to keep people alive," Bobby says.

Against every expectation, the entire O'Donnell family returned home safely. As the months went by, people would often ask Bobby, "You're going to run the Boston Marathon again, right?" But your life is not what other people want it to be. Bobby's dad was supposed to be the hero in the family. Bobby only started this journey because he wanted a jacket, and now he was genuinely afraid. "Even though finishing the Boston Marathon was a dream of mine, I was so traumatized by that day that I didn't think I would be able to do it."

It happened once. It could happen again. That's what he told himself.

One day, a few months after the tragedy, Bobby was watching some videos on YouTube. On the side of the screen, he saw a suggested video of a TED Talk called "Because I Said I Would." He clicked on it and watched a speech about the importance of keeping a promise. Bobby reflected on his own commitment to his donors, to those sick and injured children, to himself. After watching that TED Talk, Bobby came to a firm realization that he couldn't let the children's hospital suffer because of his fear.

"I'd made a promise that I would finish the race. And even though it was something that I didn't really feel comfortable doing at the time, it was a commitment that I had made," Bobby remembers.

In 2014, Bobby O'Donnell again trained for the Boston Marathon. He took a black permanent marker and wrote the words *because I said I would* on his shoes. He had a running shirt custom made with those same five words on it. On April 21, 2014, Bobby O'Donnell finished the Boston Marathon for the first time, raising $10,862 for the Boston Children's Hospital.

"We have such intentions in life," Bobby says. "We get partway down the path, but then a roadblock gets in our way, whether it's fear or discomfort, and then that's where we stop. But a promise pulls you through that wall."

There are many kinds of heroes in this world. There are the heroes who run head-on into danger to save a life, and there are the ones who quietly show up despite their fears. As I write this, Bobby is working as a paramedic and applying to medical schools: He has his sights set on becoming an emergency room doctor.

Bobby with his Mom and Dad at the finish line of the Boston Marathon

Like his dad, he wants to spend his life helping others. To this day, Bobby and Bob Senior both hand out Promise Cards to their patients in recovery, encouraging them to be stronger than their adversities.

And that massage chair that Bob Senior bought at the runner's trade expo? In all of the turmoil after the marathon, the return policy expired. Now, an overpriced Japanese massage chair sits unused in the home of a hero. ■

The Next Bed Over

Laurie's Mom Can't Shake a Thought

Laurie's mom was an alcoholic, but that habit didn't start until Laurie was about twelve or thirteen years old. Unlike some kids who have gone through a similar journey, Laurie had a chance to see what her mom was really like before things went south.

"She was kind. She was intelligent. She was determined. I remember her from when I was young, and she was the best mom ever."

When Laurie's mom grew into old age, the consequences of alcoholism caught up with her. Her liver began to fail. She frequently had to visit

Laurie and her mom

the hospital for blood transfusions and was in desperate need of a liver transplant. Eventually, Laurie's mom made it to the top of the list for the organ she needed. It was a procedure that could prolong her life and allow her to be a grandmother to Laurie's children, a second chance at life.

Laurie

But in all of this good news, there was a thought that wouldn't escape the conscience of Laurie's mom. That thought came from the hospital bed next to hers. Staying in the same room was a young boy who lived in rural Michigan. He had a terminal illness and was waiting for an entirely different organ transplant. Day in and day out, Laurie's mom would watch this child's family come into the room to take care of him. Day in and day out, she would watch them grieve.

After seeing so many of these moments, Laurie's mom began to imagine an unknown family in a far-off hospital room who was waiting for the same exact liver she needed. Over time, these thoughts became too much for her to bear.

Laurie vividly remembers her mother's words.

"Laurie, I cannot accept the liver because I have done this to myself. I cannot take that away from a family who has their whole life in front of them."

Laurie's mom believed that the time had come for her to be accountable for the decisions she had made. She refused the liver transplant and respectfully asked for her name to be taken off of the list permanently.

"She got blood transfusions for a good two years before we lost her," Laurie says. Those two years were a gift from absolute strangers—blood donors. Years later, as a New Year's resolution, Laurie decided to face a fear in memory of a mom who tried to leave the world doing what she thought was right. ∎

In 2013, I will tackle my fear of needles and donate blood for the 1st time!

because I said I would.

Jumping Out of a Plane

Moira's Promise Comes Back Six Years Later

Children rarely forget the promises you have made to them. They might forget a lot of things, but when it comes to promises, they're a steel trap. When Moira McGovern's nephew Danny (who also happened to be her godson) asked her, "Someday, will you take me skydiving? Can we jump out of a plane together?" Moira appeased him by saying, "Yeah, that would be great." Danny was only in sixth grade at that time, and Moira never thought he would hold her to it. But children believe in promises in a way that most adults have forgotten. A

Moira's nephew Danny

promise is a promise. We should mean what we say. Children are literal beings, and they have not been dulled by a lifetime of broken commitments. As adults, we teach them that lying is bad, and not enough time had passed for Danny to have forgotten that important lesson.

Moira's relationship with Danny was special to her, but their interactions were sparse. When Danny was around five years old, his mother (Moira's sister) had a pretty severe falling out with their parents. There was a lot of friction in the family, and Danny's mom broke ties. Moira was only allowed to see Danny maybe twice a year, so Moira put extra effort into these moments.

Over the years, Danny would bring up the skydiving conversation from time to time, so Moira knew it was still on his radar. In January 2014, Danny's eighteenth birthday rolled around. That was an especially important milestone—not just for all the usual reasons associated with the passage into adulthood, but also because in the state of California, where Danny grew up, you have to be at least eighteen to skydive without permission from a parent or a guardian. There was a special type of anticipation in his delight when he told Moira, "I'm legal now! We can do this."

Spelling doesn't count :)

You can imagine that Moira might also have been feeling some strong emotions right then. Most people would be afraid in this moment, because jumping out of an airplane is terrifying. But fear was not the obstacle for Moira. She did not fear jumping out of an airplane. She had a very different problem.

First-time skydivers almost always do a tandem jump physically connected to a jumpmaster—a professional skydiving instructor. Because of this, there is a skydiver weight limit of 240 pounds. Moira was significantly heavier than that. In order to make the jump, she would have to lose 50 pounds.

"I thought losing some weight in a short amount of time would be easy. I could do it with diet pills or another fast, unhealthy way," she explained to me. "What this prompted me to do was to look at the bigger picture. I was really unhappy at that point in my life. I had some depression going on, and I was in this binge-eating cycle that I could not escape." Moira paused there. "*Escape* is an interesting word, because that is what it was. I was trying to escape things that I didn't want to deal with. This became an opportunity to show up as a better person."

By her own admission, Moira has a very addictive personality. Addiction had been a part of her life since adolescence. It started with drugs and alcohol. But by Danny's eighteenth birthday, Moira had been sober for more than a year. The thing with addiction, though, is that it sometimes seems like a game of Whac-A-Mole. As soon as you defeat one addiction, another pops up. "Now my problem was eating," Moira says. "I was basically in the same behavior, just a different drug of choice—now it was sugar. I had that mindset that I wanted to put something in my body that was going to make me feel different than I do."

Moira's promise to Danny gave her the jolt she needed to see her behavior as it really was. "I was not going to be able to show up for a promise that I had made to him because I was stuck in my own addiction."

To help support her healing process, Moira talked to a psychologist who specialized in treating people through addiction and traumatic experiences. During one of their discussions, Moira's psychologist introduced her to the concept of a Promise Card. And so pen touched paper. With the decision made, a mountain of hard work still lay ahead for Moira. She was

Moira

incredibly fortunate that her boss had some health goals as well and could provide some support. "Part of my whole thing was that I didn't have time. I was working too much. My boss was in a similar situation, where she wanted to lose weight and get healthy, so she brought in a personal trainer to work with the two of us."

Her boss's personal trainer was one of those tough boot-camp types, striding in wearing a hat and a tight-fitting tank top that showed off her physique. She never let Moira get off easy. "I was supposed to be on the elliptical for ten minutes before she got there. Sometimes, that didn't happen. She would show up at my office door, and she would literally clap her hands: 'Come on, come on. Let's get up! Let's go!' She was a little militant."

Moira worked out three times a week for about a half hour in her company's little gym. Some days, Moira and her trainer would box, which she loved because it would switch up the routine a little. On the days when Moira just couldn't stand to be in the tight space of that corporate gym, they would go outside for a half-hour walk with light dumbbells.

"I wrote a promise down, and I shared it with my boss, I shared it with my trainer, I shared it with a few different helpers in my life, and then all of a sudden I had a support team who was asking me how I was doing and saying, 'Hey, do you want to go for a hike this weekend?' They were doing what they could to help me along the way."

It took six months, but with the support of the people who cared for her, Moira lost the weight required to be eligible for the jump.

On June 1, 2014, Moira drove down to Berkeley, where her nephew lived, in her black convertible Volkswagen Bug. She picked up Danny from the apartment he shared with a bunch of other guys in college, and they drove to Monterey. Monterey is an interesting place for your first jump because it has the highest tandem jump in Northern California. You leap out of a plane at eighteen thousand feet, which gives you a full ninety seconds of free fall before your parachute opens. As Moira says, "If you're going to go, go big."

Still, Moira felt no fear. Quite the opposite: "I was excited! I was so pumped to do it, and Danny was, too." She told me that the best part was actually the moment *before* the jump, the adrenaline that comes *before* you step out into nothing. With the roar of the twin engines and the rush of the wind in her ears, Moira left the safety of the cabin and stepped into the air.

Moira floated in an almost surreal silence above the water and the land, taking in the view along the coastline. What was frantic was now serene, and she says it was the most beautiful thing she has ever seen.

"I had very little faith in my own ability to keep a promise to myself or

to somebody else because I had failed so many times," Moira says, reflecting on the experience.

We would all love to say that we have unlimited drive and determination to fulfill our commitments, but sometimes we simply don't. I'm not addressing Moira here: I am talking to you, the reader of this book, and I am holding up the mirror to myself as well. We can't always do it alone. Sometimes, we need a good boss or a militant trainer. Sometimes, the equation requires more than just one. Do not underestimate the importance of an accountability partner in your promise. It is not a mark against your character to need support. If anything, it is the opposite. It is a sign of good character when you are humble enough to ask for help. No one is above having an accountability partner, especially when it comes to keeping a promise to a child. ■

A Single Piece of Notebook Paper

Founder of because I said I would Quits His Job

It has been a very interesting experience being behind something that went viral. Maybe, like many people out there, I assumed that when you go viral, money just starts pouring out of the walls. Right? I mean, there was once a guy who started a crowdfunding project to make potato salad that raised $55,492. It wasn't some celebrity chef. No recently unearthed ancient potato salad recipe. The fundraising goal was literally set at $10, and the entire campaign's description was, "Basically I'm just making potato salad. I haven't decided what kind yet."

$55,492.

With stories like this one as my context, when *because I said I would* first went viral, I naturally thought that the cost of printing and mailing Promise Cards would be covered by the generosity of strangers. I figured I just had to keep volunteering my time to send these things, and the universe would take care of the financial side.

That did not happen. Donations were not covering costs at all. Not even close. I had two choices:

1. Stop sending Promise Cards to people for free

2. Put my money where my mouth is

To keep the promise I made to all of these Internet strangers, I ended up spending over $20,000 of my paychecks and savings to buy paper,

This is me, the author of the book you're reading right now. Hi.

stamps, envelopes, and other supplies. I had just lost my father, and I wasn't about to let *because I said I would* die without a fight.

At the time, I had the benefit of having a great salary that helped me fund *because I said I would* independently. I was the youngest manager at an enterprise software company listed as one of *Fortune*'s 100 Best Companies to Work For in the United States. I had stock options. I made five-figure bonuses. I just had to keep going to work, shovel the money over to *because I said I would*, count cards at night, and hope that it would all turn around one day.

Leaving my job made absolutely no sense financially. But one day, I was pushed over the edge emotionally by a letter that was dropped off at my desk. I read it, and I knew it was time for me to go. It was February 2013. I must have just come back from lunch or a meeting when I saw a sealed envelope sitting at my desk that hadn't been there before. There was no address on it. No postmarking of any kind. It didn't say who it was from. It just said *Alex Sheen* in blue marker. I opened the envelope and this is what I read:

Feb. 2013

hi alex.

I have been keeping up with your blog...Because I said I would has really really helped me through a rough patch. There have been lots of times where I didn't think life was worth living, and I almost took my life. almost. I am getting stronger everyday, + a lot of that strength comes from a few Promise cards I have written. I have lots of people who care about me, I am a very, very lucky person. It took a lot for me to realize that I SHOULD be alive, I DO have a purpose. I'm not sure if I would even be around if it wasn't for you and your organization. So, thanks, Mr. Sheen. I know I am supposed to write this on a card... but I want to promise YOU that I will not give up. & I hope that one day I can

I sat at my desk that day and cried, reading this letter. I thought about what my father might say about a promise like that. I stood up in my office, in the sea of people, and I wondered, *Who is it? Is this a friend of mine who doesn't want me to know what they are going through so they left their name off it? Or is this a complete stranger?* There were 1,300 people that worked at the company; I couldn't know them all.

This letter gave me the courage to do what I already knew had to be done. It was time to leave the comfort of my job and work to ensure the long-term survival of this cause. I was already bleeding money, but this letter let me know that it was time to really gamble. No more half in, half out. If that meant that I had to go down with the ship, then so be it.

I decided to email my boss and request a meeting. I was vague in my message, so she didn't know what this meeting was about, but she agreed to it. With the letter in hand, I walked into her office. I handed the letter to her and said, "Hey, boss. If you could just read this letter, it would make it a lot easier for me to do what I've got to do right now."

"Sure, Alex. No problem," she said.

She unfolded the college-ruled piece of notebook paper and began to read.

Last photo of me taken as an employee in the office at the software company

But then she stopped. She had this look on her face that I had never seen before, and I have not seen since. She looked up at me.

"Alex, this letter . . . this letter is from my daughter. This is her handwriting. This is about her, and that envelope you're holding—that's the kind of envelope we have on our kitchen counter. When did she give this to you?"

I couldn't believe what she was saying. I mean that literally. For a second, I thought she was joking, but clearly she would not joke about something like that. The letter I used to tell my boss I needed to quit was written by her own child.

My boss's daughter was suffering from depression. She was fourteen years old. She was overweight, and other kids picked on her. In the complexity of the human condition, perhaps the worst feeling is loneliness. At such a young age, she didn't know what to do with her emotions and began cutting herself.

My boss introduced the idea of Promise Cards to her daughter. Her daughter used them to write out some promises that she thought would help end her habit of self-harm. This young girl is part of the reason you are reading this book right now. I quit my job to help people in need, and I am never going back. ■

The because I said I would
Code Of Honor

··

What does it mean to live with honor? That is a hard question to answer, but knowing the definition of the word *honor* can be a good place to start. *Merriam-Webster's Collegiate Dictionary* has not just one meaning for *honor*, or two, but *ten* different definitions. One entry defines honor as "a keen sense of ethical conduct."[1] But what is ethical? Go to the definition of *ethic* and read the words *moral duty*. But what morals deserve a sense of duty?

---

1   *Merriam-Webster's Collegiate Dictionary*, 11th ed. 2009, s. v. "honor."

The dictionary does not define these words with any specific character values. They are not defined by empathy, loyalty, honesty, or kindness. The word *honor* is only an empty framework where character values have yet to be determined. But how many people have actually defined for themselves what it means to live an honorable life? Ask a room of a hundred random people, "Who here has written out a personal code of honor?" Seeing even a couple raised hands would be surprising.

Developing a personal code of honor is an incredibly simple and undervalued exercise that can affect our lives positively every single day. Many moments in life carry the burden of moral ambiguity where the best decision is not clear.

Should I tell the truth, even though it will hurt someone's feelings?

Should I intervene in this inappropriate argument between two strangers?

When holding my daughter accountable for her actions, at what point have I gone too far?

Without a code of honor, our actions can be misguided by the temporary and sometimes irrational emotions of a particular moment. Not having a personal code of honor is like a courtroom run by a judge in a country with no laws—verdicts are as inconsistent as the weather, and the decisions vary day by day. The fate of a life is decided by impulse instead of integrity.

To word it differently, a personal code of honor is more accurately described as a filter for life's decisions. Bad decisions are evaluated by the code and they fail to pass through the filter, never entering our reality. Good decisions meet the standard and are chosen with purpose.

The benefits of a personal code of honor are numerous: less hesitation, less regret, more respect from others, more respect for yourself, and the list goes on. Organizations can also benefit from a code of honor, and that is why one was developed to help guide *because I said I would* on its journey. To select these principles, we turned to the people who built it: our supporters. The process of creating our code of honor started by organizing some of these compelling stories into groups based on common characteristics and then naming each group after a single characteristic. I consulted with our staff and many of our supporters, and eventually these groupings were boiled down to seven elements, which became known as the *because I said I would* Code of Honor:

1. Self-Control
2. Compassion
3. Contemplation
4. Honesty
5. Accountability
6. Sacrifice
7. Hope

This book contains seven sections that individually describe each of these elements of honor. These text-only chapters will hopefully provide you with a practical perspective on each topic that can be applied to your life. Please note that the promise stories featured *between* these Code of Honor chapters do not relate solely to any one element of honor. Why? Most promises strongly represent *multiple* elements of honor, not just one. To label each of these stories with only one element would be confusing because much of that is up to the reader's personal interpretation. Each collection of stories between the elements of honor sections should be seen as random.

And even though I am very passionate about these principles and I have adopted them as a personal code of honor, I urge you to create your own. Organize the people, the stories, and the experiences in your life into themed groups. Name these groups with a defined character value. No soft words. Don't select words that you just think sound good. Make sure you mean what you say. Our Code of Honor might be a good starting place for this process, but it shouldn't be the end. It is important for each of us to establish a personal code of honor for ourselves. We all have the awesome privilege and responsibility of determining who we want to be. I hope only the best for you on that journey. ∎

Self-Control

THE GREATEST BATTLE LIES WITHIN

....

If you could press a button and make every twelve-year-old child (an entire generation) 10 percent better at any one thing, what would it be? Phrased differently, what one characteristic do you want (or would you want) your child to be born with? Many people naturally lean toward answering that type of question with skills or abilities that would inherently help their child to face life's adversities. We know that life is not fair because we have lived it. We have seen the hardships and the tragedies. When we think about our children, we worry about the monsters that may come for them.

Maybe the monster that comes will be a disease, so we teach our kids about nutrition and exercise. But maybe the monster is not a physical battle. Maybe the monster will be poverty, so we educate our children so they can secure a job and take care of themselves and their future families. Or perhaps the monster will be a tragic accident, so we teach them about danger and safety procedures. The unfortunate fact is that we do not know which monster (or monsters) is coming. Worry as we will, the future is unknown.

Nevertheless, let's still ask the question: What one characteristic do you (or would you) want your child to be born with? There are many great answers, but I believe perhaps one characteristic may prepare a child for life better than any other: self-control. Self-control wakes you up at 7:00 in the morning to exercise even if you're tired. With self-control, you study hard even when you weren't born adept at the subject. Self-control buckles the seatbelt even if it's uncomfortable. Self-control is perhaps the only characteristic that gives you a chance to fight all the monsters.

But how much self-control is based on an individual's choice and how much is genetics? Are people like Bobby O'Donnell, the Boston marathon runner, genetically predisposed to have more self-control than other people? That may sound a little unconventional, but let's consider a more specific example of self-control that has been scientifically researched: alcoholism. The National

Institute on Alcohol Abuse and Alcoholism believes that genetic predisposition accounts for half of the risk in developing Alcohol Use Disorder. Scientific research concludes that children of alcoholics are approximately four times more likely than the general population to develop alcohol problems.[2]

With these facts in mind, would it be too far-fetched to say that there is a genetic predisposition for self-control at large? I don't think that's crazy. However, I don't believe that this solidifies our destiny either. The odds may sometimes be against us, but I have seen the odds beaten time and time again. Self-control is a muscle that can be trained and developed. Practice is required. We can't expect to lie under 300 pounds and bench-press it on our first attempt. Self-control develops slowly, built one repetition at a time.

Consider intentionally challenging yourself in small ways on a daily basis. One way to do that is to view minor frustrating moments in your life as opportunities for personal development. Let's say you lock your keys in your car, which will probably make you late for work. It's easy to boil over with frustration and anger in this moment. At times like this, I ask myself, *If I can't handle even this moment with self-control, how am I going to have self-control when it really matters?* This is what I do:

- Take three deep breaths.

- Remember my code of honor.

- Tell myself out loud what I know is best to do in this moment.

Thankfully, life provides a lot of these moments for practice. Wait ten minutes before you send that angry text message. Try to understand that the person that just cut you off in traffic makes mistakes

2   "A Family History of Alcoholism: Are You At Risk?," National Institute on Alcohol Abuse and Alcoholism, June 2012, https://pubs.niaaa.nih.gov/publications/FamilyHistory/fambist.htm

just like everyone else. You will not have to search for these types of moments. They will come to you.

Another way to build self-control is to *purposefully* put yourself in situations of discomfort. You see people do this all the time with marathon running. We can put ourselves through a test, and when we are finished, we forever benefit from a new mental strength that says, *If I can do that, then I can do this.* But there are more mundane challenges you can purposefully pursue that will benefit your self-control. For example, I am right-handed, but sometimes I use my left hand to brush my teeth. Or I will tie my shoes with one hand for no reason. Sometimes I take a cold shower, even though the hot water is working just fine. I create these moments of frustration to build a mindset that accepts and overcomes challenges, even if I create those moments myself.

Before this book's release, if you were to ask 1,000 of our supporters to sum up the philosophy of *because I said I would* in a single word, many would offer terms like *integrity, determination,* or *perseverance.* But when you boil down these words to their elements, you find that they all point to *self-control.* And while there are stories in this book about astonishing acts of self-control, please do not take them as a suggestion that we all need to become superhuman. Yes, climbing Mount Everest makes for a cool story, but in all honesty, do we all really need to do that? What we actually need is just enough self-control to become a better version of ourselves.

A 10 percent change in self-control could be the difference between a kid studying enough to graduate or missing the grades and becoming another dropout. In the moment right before a teen shoplifts, 10 percent more self-control could change the trajectory of their entire future. We would love for the world to make some wholesale changes, but maybe just 10 percent might be enough to change the course of human history forever. ∎

CODE OF HONOR:

Self-Control

—

My greatest battle lies within. Control over one's own emotions, desires, and actions often defines the success or the failure of a promise. I work to build self-control so that I may better myself and the world around me.

because I said I would.

because
I said
I would.

STORY COLLECTION #2

I promise to be as strong as I know I have the potential to be. I promise to stay the course, to be diligent and honor myself. I promise that despite any urge, I will not buy <u>one</u> more pack of cigarettes.

because I said I would.

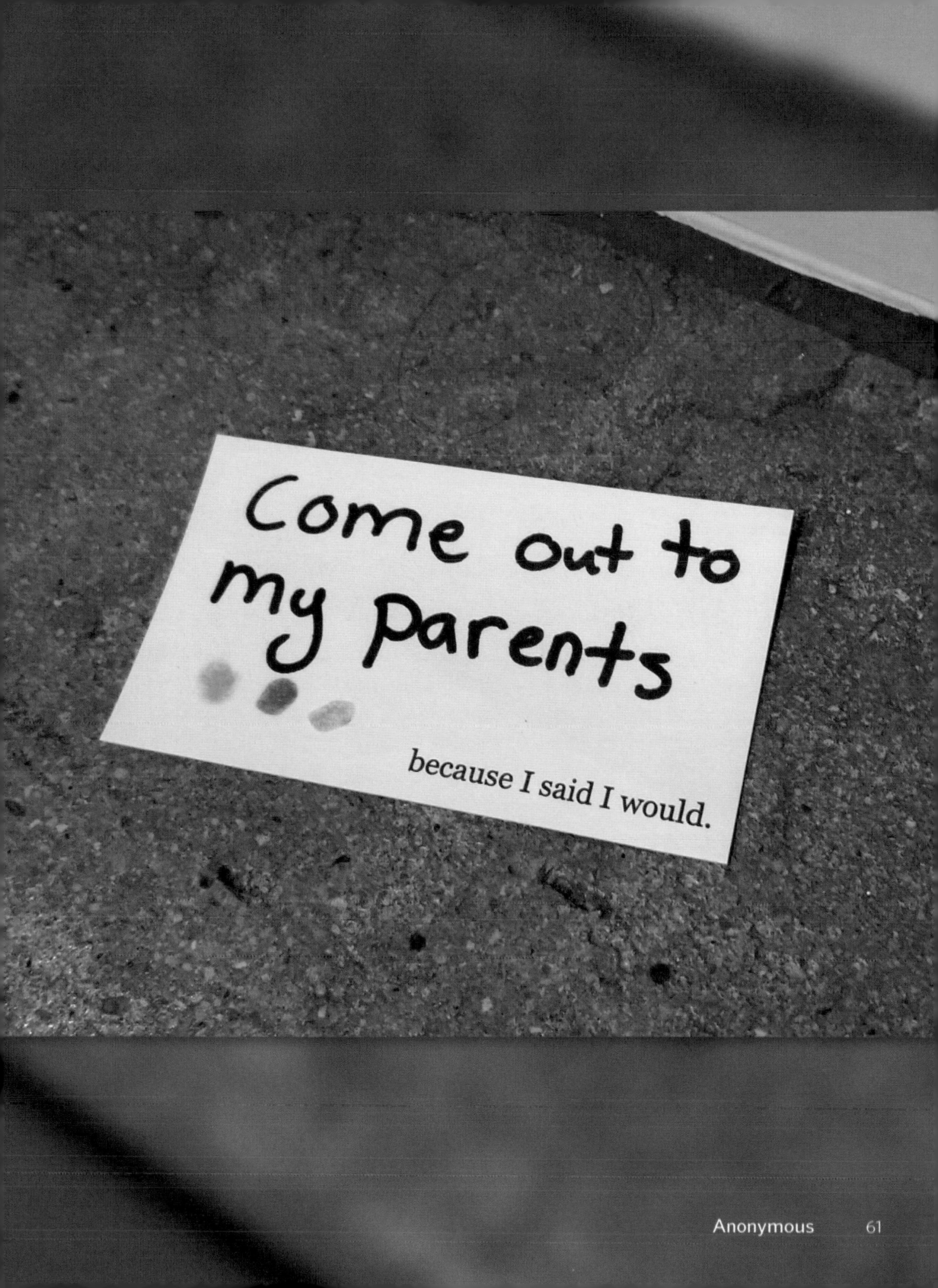
Come out to my parents
because I said I would.

◀ Love for the cause
shared on Instagram.

I will become
a hospice
volunteer

Christine   because I said I would.

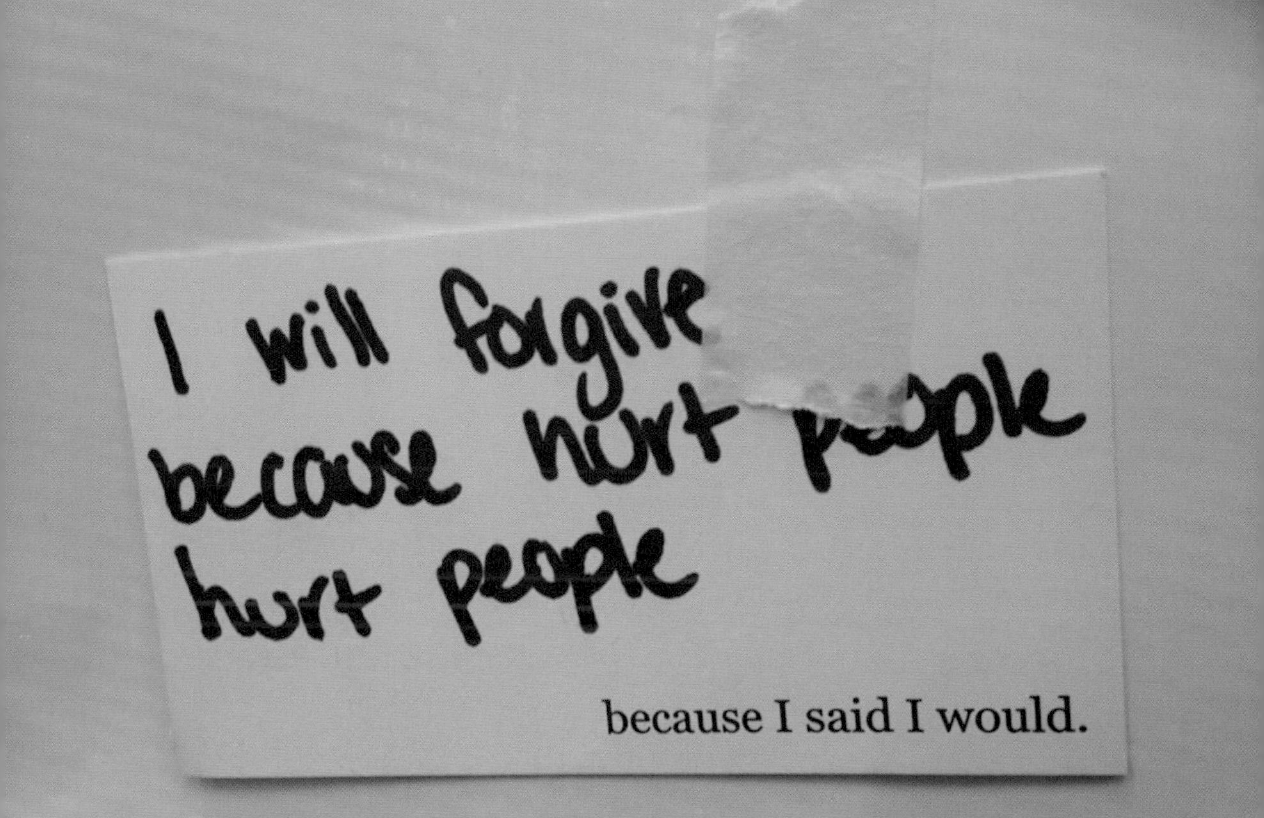

I will forgive
because hurt people
hurt people

because I said I would.

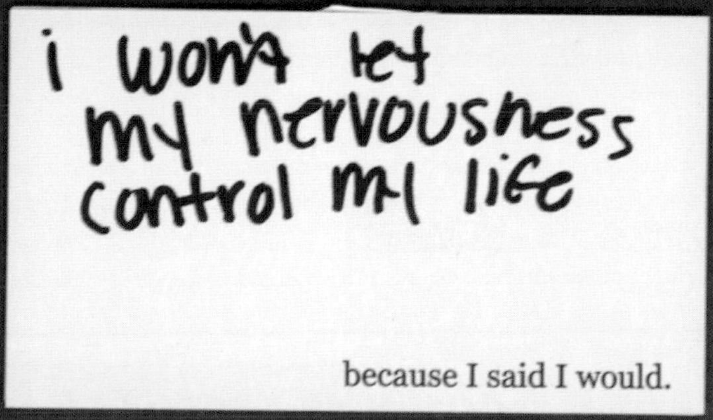

i won't let
my nervousness
control my life

because I said I would.

" I HAVE AORTIC STENOSIS with a bicuspid valve, and I've always seen a cardiologist. I had open-heart surgery five years ago, and it really changed my life. I've always known that, eventually, I was going to have to have my aortic valve replaced because it was bad.

It's a bicuspid, which means it's normally three leaflets, but mine had only two leaflets, and I always knew this was going to happen eventually.

I didn't have control of really anything concerning my health, so I would do things like overeat or other things that weren't very good for me because I had control over that. I let this behavior spiral out of control, and so that's why I am overweight now.

▲ Excerpts from a video recorded by Joel. He lost 30 pounds within three months of recording this message.

I realize I'm fat, and I'm not okay with that anymore. It's not fair to my family and my friends, who care about me. So I decided to make a change. As of today, I'm down forty pounds. I decided to make a conscious change to eat better, so I'll be around in the future for my friends and family.

Average people can do extraordinary things. I'm an average person. I'm meant to do something extraordinary. Everyone can do something great. It's in here. It's deep down. They just have to unlock it.

How is it fair for me to let my life spiral out of control and eat whatever I want and make unhealthy decisions? I could be making a change. I could be helping someone. I could be making a difference in someone else's life. How is it fair for me to rob that person out there, who needs me—how is that fair? That's not fair.

So I decided to make a change, and it's been difficult, but I continue to remind myself what I'm working for. It's for me, but it's also for everyone. It's for my friends. It's for my family whom I love and I care about. It's for people I don't know yet. It's for my future spouse. It's for my future kids. I'm thinking for the future.

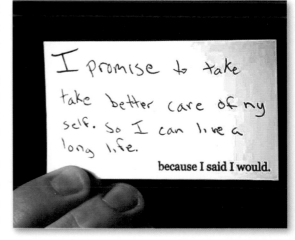

I promise to my friends and family that I will take better care of myself and eat healthier, continue to lose weight, and encourage others to live a healthy lifestyle."

▲ **AMANDA BERRY, GINA DEJESUS, AND LILY ROSE LEE** (formerly known as Michelle Knight) were kidnapped and held captive in a Cleveland, Ohio, house for over ten years. I made a promise to them that I would walk over 240 miles across the entire state of Ohio to raise funding for their recovery and to raise awareness for victims of sexual violence. On June 25, 2013, that walk ended at 2207 Seymour Avenue, Cleveland, Ohio. Gina DeJesus's mother was the first person to give me a hug when I finished. I will remember that moment forever.

Twenty Tours
in the Middle East

Colonel Parker Schenecker Never Stops Being a Dad

This story begins on January 28, 2011. It's 9:58 p.m. local time, and Colonel Parker Schenecker, age forty-eight, is sitting in a secure facility in the country of Qatar. There are no windows in the entire building. The entry and exit are secured via badge and access codes, with armed police at each door.

Colonel Parker Schenecker is an intelligence officer in the United States Army. He has served in the army for twenty-seven years, including twenty deployments in the Middle East. On this particular evening,

he is on a deployment to Afghanistan, making a stop in Qatar as part of his assignment. He is sitting in an office, preparing for a secure video teleconference with United States Central Command headquarters, located in Tampa, Florida, which he also calls home. As he is organizing his materials for this meeting, he looks up and sees two officers in battle dress walking toward his desk. One is an army colonel, and the other is a captain in the United States Air Force.

"I looked up at them, and I thought

they were teammates who were going to talk about what had happened that day or missions they needed us to support," the colonel remembers, reflecting on this night. As the two officers continued to walk toward him from far across the room, Parker looks down at his desk, and in that split second, he realized why they were there. This situation was eerily similar to what is described in the US Army Casualty program.

Army Regulation 600-8-1 specifies the protocol used to notify service members when someone in their family has become ill, has been injured, or has died. It stipulates that two uniformed service members—one an officer of the same rank, out of respect for the circumstances—will deliver the information face-to-face. As Colonel Schenecker looks at these officers, he knows the intent of their visit before they even utter a word. He thinks it is about his mother. Colonel Schenecker's mom is in her seventies, and he understood the natural course of life. He is prepared to hear that his mother has passed away.

But that is not what he is told.

The two officers inform Colonel Parker Schenecker that his wife shot and killed their only two children. Julie Schenecker picked up their thirteen-year-old son, Beau, from soccer practice and drove him home. As they were sitting in the car together, Julie pulled out a handgun and shot her son in the head. When she arrived at their home, she walked inside. Her daughter, Calyx, age sixteen, was sitting at her desk doing homework. Calyx's life ended in that moment.

Colonel Schenecker received directions for his flight path home. From the Middle East, he would fly on commercial airlines to Washington, DC, and then on to Tampa. People could see that he was a uniformed officer in the army as he walked through the crowds from airport to airport. What was invisible to them were the thoughts in his mind that no man should ever have to carry.

Calyx and Beau Schenecker

While Colonel Schenecker struggled to make sense of what happened, he was also burdened with the wider-reaching scope of the situation. "Not only did I have the responsibility to get myself through this, but I also had the responsibility to get all of [Calyx and Beau's] friends through this," he told me. These children were experiencing loss for the first time, and Colonel Schenecker felt that it was his duty to lead them.

Calyx and Beau's funeral was held on Tuesday, February 8, 2011. The gruesome circumstances of his children's deaths had attracted relentless news coverage. The media's sole focus was on the nature of the murders. Journalists wanted to know what type of gun was used, they wanted to talk to the killer, and they wanted photos. When was someone going to ask, "What made each of these kids special?"

On top of the news coverage that no father would want to see, Colonel Schenecker was told that the Westboro Baptist Church, a hate group widely known for its inflammatory speech against US soldiers, the LGBT community, Catholics, and others, would be protesting outside his children's memorial service. On that day, Colonel Schenecker gathered himself and prepared for a different type of battle. He walked up to a church podium to talk about his children.

"I can't thank you enough for today's loving and moving memorial for my exceptional children, and for your tributes through the past few days.

Whether you wore some blue or some Harry Potter glasses, whether you lit a candle, laid a flower, or signed a soccer jersey, you honored my children. Your devoted friend. Your classmate. Your teammate. My family and I are humbled by your support, grace, and overwhelming love for Calyx and Beau. They love you too. Please don't forget how they lived."

To Colonel Schenecker, Calyx and Beau were still alive in the hearts and minds of their friends. He would do his best to sustain that life. And so, in front of an international audience, in what he considers the most important promise he will ever make—even more important than a soldier's oath of enlistment—he affirmed, "Today, we celebrate how they lived, and I will spend the rest of my time doing just that."

In the months following his children's deaths, Colonel Schenecker established the Calyx and Beau Schenecker Memorial Fund. Beau loved soccer, so the fund provides grants to sponsor statewide soccer tournaments. Calyx loved art, so the memorial fund holds a high school fine arts competition every year in her name. The Calyx and Beau Schenecker Memorial Fund promotes the arts, athletics, and altruism, supporting today's young people by giving them a chance to live their dreams. It has provided more than $70,000 in scholarships for students and grants for nonprofit organizations.

As children in a military family, Calyx and Beau had to move a lot from city to city, following their father's career; they had a deep compassion and empathy for what it was like to be the new kids in town. To impart the love and kindness that his children had for others, Colonel Schenecker started a speaker series for ethics and leadership in their memory. I was honored to be the inaugural speaker.

Some time after that speech, Colonel Schenecker joined the *because I said I would* staff to help start our chapter program. After his time on staff with us, he continued as a volunteer at a local *because I said I would* chapter, serving as a chapter leader for a full year, as he said he would.

In all my conversations with this incredible human being, there was one concept Parker shared with me that I find especially hard to grasp.

"My story would have been just as unthinkable if my children had died in a car accident. How they died is irrelevant to my promise story," he said.

You may find it difficult to understand that thought as I once did. Unfortunately, the horrific nature of the circumstances draws our attention to the actions and motives of Calyx and Beau's mother. It took some time to put Parker's perspective in context, but eventually I came to a realization: *The loss of your children is so terribly saddening that their absence cannot be overshad-*

owed by anything, and that even includes how they passed or who killed them. The simple fact is that they are gone. Nothing else really matters.

Many people are curious how Colonel Schenecker continues to live in the wake of these events. At a *because I said I would* event in 2014, he addressed that thought in his own way.

"The question isn't how I do it. The real question is, *How will you do it?* When life knocks you down to your knees, will you stay down? Will you hope that the ref just counts to ten? Five. Six. Seven. Eight.

"Will you throw in the towel, or will you pick up that towel, and wipe off the sweat, and wipe off the blood, and dry the tears, and wipe away the fear, and live? I think you guys know my choice." ■

The Optional Assignment

Mrs. Newberry Has an Idea

Amie Newberry's husband, Kevin, is a pilot for Southwest Airlines. Among the many perks that come along with that job, there is an odd one that Amie loves maybe the most. "I love their in-flight magazines, and he often brings them home for me to read. Actually, he does every month."

In November 2013, Amie boarded a plane to New Mexico to meet up with her husband. As soon as she sat down on the plane, she reached into the back pocket of the seat in front of her and pulled out the in-flight magazine with a nerdy sense of anticipation. On the cover of this magazine was a phrase that caught her attention: *because I said I would*. The magazine chose to interview us for their feature story for the month.

Unlike some passengers, Amie was not just reading this article to fill the time between takeoff and landing. Amie uses personal interest articles in the classroom. At the time, she was teaching sophomore honors English, senior English, and Advanced Placement language and composition at McQueen High School in Reno, Nevada. She believes that English is the perfect channel to teach real-life lessons.

Amie and her husband

After reading about *because I said I would* in that magazine, Amie Newberry created a unique assignment in which she challenges her students to write an English essay about an important promise they need to make and keep in their life. The hope was to create a thought-provoking and challenging moment for the kids. The importance of a promise can be taught, even in a classroom.

But here's the catch: Amie gives her students the option *not* to do the promise essay assignment. She offers them an alternative assignment that they can complete if they don't want to take the Promise Cards. "I don't want them to feel like, 'Oh, I've got to do these stupid cards.' I want it to be authentic."

Not a single one of her students has ever chosen to do the alternative work.

In her first year, Amie started the assignment by printing out 5,000 Promise Cards using a template that is freely available on our website (becauseisaidiwould.com/printcards). She used money out of her own pocket to print these copies locally. Unfortunately, the average teacher in the United States spends nearly $500 of his or her own money for classroom materials each year, according to the Education Market Association.[3] We often mail Promise Cards to teachers at no cost, but Amie wanted to cover the cost personally.

Not only were the cards used by Mrs. Newberry's students, but also she created a massive Promise Wall in the hallway where every student in the entire school could write and publicly share their commitments. The wall became such a conversation piece that students who didn't even have Amie as a teacher visited her classroom between periods to ask if they could have some cards.

"Twenty years from now, my students will never remember if they had a vocabulary list with twenty words or what those words were," Amie says. "What they will remember is if we create an experience in the classroom

---

3   Martha C. White, "Here's How Much Your Kid's Teacher Is Shelling Out for School Supplies," *Money*, August 3, 2016, time.com/money/4392319/teachers-buying-school-supplies/.

that applies to life, and somehow causes an internal shift or change. We can plant a seed that comes to fruition later."

Because I said I would offers resources that help plant those seeds of change Amie mentioned. We have created character education lesson plans, activity ideas, videos, and other materials that are freely available to educators on our website (becauseisaidiwould.com/charactereducation). Thank you to all the teachers out there who believe that building a strong generation requires more than standardized testing. ■

This is an excerpt from a promise essay written by Alyssa, a student in Mrs. Newberry's class.

"Newbs, this part is for you. Thank you so much for assigning this project and this essay. Writing this essay made me cry, which as I stated before, is typical, but it also made me smile. It made me sad, but it also made me excited.

"The definition of a promise is as follows: a declaration or assurance that one will do a particular thing or that a particular thing will happen. With these cards, and from you and your class, I have learned the value of a promise and the value of the words we speak.

"Thank you for all the things you have taught me; thank you for assigning these cards. The because I said I would project is influential and successful, and I couldn't be happier after doing it. I love my life, I love my friends, I love my family, and I love everything that this assignment has taught me, because it is so much more than a school assignment. Thank you for redefining an English class and teaching me what I know I will never learn from another teacher. You are so much more than an English teacher; you are one of the most amazing people I have ever met.

"I love you, and thank you."

The Rom-Com Does It Again

Matt Meets Nicole

Matt Savage is an awesome name. The guy who owns that name is six-foot-four and 260 pounds, so the *Savage* part kind of fits. Matt is now thirty-six years old, but back in the day, throwing a baseball for him was as easy as ringing a bell. He was a pitcher at the University of North Carolina at Charlotte. He didn't throw the fastest ball, but Matt's pitches had movement that left a lot of batters swinging at the wind. After playing in college for four years, the game would come to an end, and it was time to enter the real world. Matt graduated and moved back to his hometown of Oklahoma City, Oklahoma. In 2005,

Matt was at home, sitting in front of his computer cruising Myspace. (Before Facebook's wild popularity, Myspace was the ruling king of social media.) Matt was looking at the profile of a family friend when he noticed someone on his friend's list of friends. In the warm glow of the computer monitor, a picture of a girl named Nicole caught

Matt's eye. In fairness to Matt, Nicole is very pretty. He read her profile and messaged their mutual friend to learn more about her. It felt somewhat like a seventh grader passing a note about a girl to his friend in the hallway between classes.

As Matt was telling me the story of how he came across Nicole, he said, "I mean, you know me. I don't always have the best choice of words."

How right he is.

Matt would eventually send a message directly to Nicole on Myspace. His first message was: "Hey, I heard you have dated a few baseball players, and I wanted to let you know that I'm a baseball player."

I wish I could have been inside Matt's head when he decided that would be the best line to start with. Who am I to judge, though, because it worked! Nicole agreed to go to a movie with him. Matt picked her up in his 1996 GMC pickup truck on a December night in Oklahoma. They went to see a rom-com featuring Kevin Costner. From that evening in the movie theater, their love would grow, and they would eventually get married. Kevin Costner, if you're reading this: Good job. You did it, man.

In 2014, living in Denver, Colorado, Matt and Nicole agreed that they both wanted to have a baby. After several months of trying, though, pregnancy tests kept coming back negative. They decided to see a fertility specialist, who recommended they try intrauterine insemination. Seven rounds and more than a year later, there were no positive results. In March 2016, they decided to attempt a different procedure called in vitro fertilization. When Nicole went in for the egg retrieval, the results looked good: ten or twelve eggs. But it still didn't work. They tried again. On the second round, there was just one egg and no success. In September 2016, sitting there in the doctor's office, they were told that if they wanted children, they should consider adopting.

Matt explains, "She has no control over it. It is not her fault." I could hear in his voice how he felt about his wife and the misplaced guilt she had. Even though she had no reason to, Nicole felt as if she had failed. Matt just wanted her to know that he didn't blame her.

There was so much pain around their unfulfilled desire for a family that it took them a few months before they could sit down and talk about it more deeply. When that conversation eventually happened, Matt and Nicole decided to set aside their plans for a family and look at things a little differently.

"Let's find something else to fill our time with and still have fun and enjoy life," they said.

Coincidentally, around the time of their decision to move forward in life without children, Matt heard about *because I said I would* in a speech that I delivered in Boston. In that speech, I mentioned that we had already started a local chapter of *because I said I would* in Denver. Matt and Nicole started attending local chapter meetups and taking part in our promises to help others in need.

Local *because I said I would* chapters keep promises to help people in need and work to become better citizens through personal development. Each month our chapters complete a volunteer project and, by supporting different causes, we offer our chapter members an opportunity to see a range of issues affecting their city. Matt has given blood, helped construct

housing for low-income families, sewn comfort pillows for autistic children, and so much more. Keeping promises to others is important, but what about addressing personal challenges, goals, and promises? To help with that side of life, our chapters hold personal development workshops that teach new topics each month. By learning things like time management best practices, the psychology of motivation, and other topics, we are better able to keep the promises we make, even the ones we make to ourselves.

Through our chapter, Matt saw a part of life that he had not fully witnessed before. Like many Americans, Matt had volunteered maybe once a year for a charitable cause through his company, but that's nothing like what he's done in the chapter. He's met new people and grew from their perspectives and support.

While talking on the phone about his experiences, Matt told me that he just completed a volunteer project. The Denver chapter of *because I said I would* made a promise to feed the homeless. They had bought, prepared, and served 140 lunches and then distributed them downtown to people in need. "I actually had tears in my eyes. I don't know why. I just looked around and saw people in this situation, and it was heartbreaking. We came together as a group that day. It was an extremely powerful moment for me."

Matt and Nicole found a way to take a difficult situation in their lives and turn it into something better for others. Love has a funny way of doing that.

I still can't believe that Myspace pickup line worked. ∎

The Youngest of Five

Amanda Messer Is the Baby

Jesse looks like he would drive a van with a mural of a majestic bald eagle playing the bass guitar painted on the side. He's an older rock-and-roll kind of guy, rough around the edges. When a lot of men like Jesse think about having kids, they think about having sons. Not Jesse. As a young man, Jesse really wanted to have a daughter. How bad? He just kept trying until he got one. That's how Amanda Messer ended up with four older brothers. Amanda, Jesse's only daughter and youngest child, was born on January 18, 1987.

Amanda grew up as a member of a big family in a small house. She always felt left out from her brothers. "Who wants to play with their little sister, right?" Amanda says as she reflects on her childhood. She is naturally introverted and has felt like a bit of an outcast at times. Amanda got picked on at school sometimes, but she never felt she needed many friends—perhaps just a few good ones.

Amanda and her dad

Maybe for these reasons, no one has ever made Amanda feel more loved than her father. Jesse has always listened when Amanda is talking and he has never pressured her to be someone she's not. He has always accepted her for who she is. When Amanda was growing up, she would stay up late watching movies with her dad. If she got into a fight with her mom, she would flee to her dad's arms.

For everything that Jesse did right as a parent, unfortunately, Amanda's father was not good at keeping his promises. He had great intentions, but sometimes intentions are not enough. Jesse would often promise to be there for his daughter—maybe it was something as simple as picking Amanda up from her mom's house. On these days, as a little girl, she would wait by the window, and time would pass with no sign of him. Crying, she would ask her mom, "Can't we call him again?" But Amanda's mom knew that it didn't matter how many times they called. Her dad wasn't going to show up. Her mom understood something that her little girl could not yet understand. Amanda's dad was an alcoholic and drug addict. He had been convicted of drunk driving over ten times.

Amanda and her dad

When someone you love doesn't keep their promises, it hurts in a way that is hard to describe. Although her dad may have been more fun than her mom, over time, Amanda realized that her mom was the one who was truly reliable, even if they didn't get along all the time. Perhaps because of her father, Amanda grew up finding it hard to trust people.

Amanda and her son, Trent

Eventually, Amanda had a child of her own. Out of the pain of broken promises that Amanda felt with her father, she swore to herself that her own son, Trent, would never experience that type of pain because of her. She wanted him to grow up and be a man of his word. To give him the greatest chance of doing that, she knew that she must lead by example.

One day in 2012, Amanda was sitting at home when she saw a post on social media made by a friend and coworker who was going through hard times. The post was about family and what it meant to be there for one another. The words brought back emotions

from Amanda's childhood. She felt compelled to do something.

Amanda was looking at my Facebook page the day I lost my father.

She is the cofounder of *because I said I would*.

Amanda worked at Hyland Software, the same software company where I worked, and that's where we met. When my father died, she was the very first person to make a post on the Facebook page for *because I said I would* and has been our strongest supporter since that day.

Don't get me wrong: There were many people who helped along the way in those first couple years. Please understand that I appreciate their support. My friends and family who offered a few hours here and there made a huge difference. But Amanda was the only one who stayed up night after night. She is the only one who left her job to ensure our existence. There was only one person who believed in this movement enough to do what was needed for *because I said I would* to survive, and her name is Amanda Messer.

I cannot explain to you the level of debt that I feel to Amanda. In the first year after my father passed, I was in pain. I missed my dad. I still miss him today, but back then my emotions were raw; I would cry alone at night. As I tried to start this effort in honor of his greatest quality, I was bleeding money. People who cared about me said that my hopes for this nonprofit were delusional and that I should just keep my corporate job, which other people would be grateful to have. I would have had to face these doubts alone if it were not for Amanda. While there may have been a slim chance that *because I said I would* could have become what it is today without her, I would bet my house that it would not have.

It is somehow fitting that our cofounder and I had opposite life experiences. Many of our supporters tend to appreciate our cause because of one of two distinct reasons: Their lives were changed by someone who (1) kept their promises or (2) someone who did not.

I know Amanda's father personally, and please know that he is a very nice guy. I think a lot of people (including me) struggle in separating an addiction from a person. Even with all the disappointment, Amanda still loves her father dearly. Jesse has had spells of sobriety along the way and is currently on an incredible stretch of abstinence from alcohol. We both hope that he can continue on this path.

As we grew to know each other, Amanda and I started dating. In a professional sense, that is somewhat uncomfortable to write, because she is the cofounder and chief technology officer of *because I said I would*. But I guess that many charities start with close-knit relationships like ours was. Maybe it is a husband and wife, or two family members, who believe in a cause enough to fight for it together.

Perhaps my greatest regret in the journey of *because I said I would* is that I have not given more credit to Amanda and her contributions to this cause. I should have recognized her more. The truth is that I get too much credit for building something that could not have been built alone.

If you find yourself in a leadership role, do not make the same mistake that I have made. Do not forget about that one person who was there for you when no one else was.

Who, in the midst of your greatest challenge, gave you a hug when you needed it the most? Who looked you squarely in the eye and told you that you were stronger than you believed? Make sure that person knows who they are and what they mean to you. Do not let another day go by without saying it.

Amanda Messer, thank you for everything you have done for me and for countless people around the world who needed you. ■

Promise Cards in Prison

Changing Lives from Behind Bars

Of all the Promise Cards that have been distributed around the world, more than one million of them have been counted and packed by inmates at the Lorain Correctional Institution (LCI), a maximum-security prison for men located about thirty miles west of Cleveland, Ohio. At LCI, they offer a range of programs to help inmates, such as classes for anger management or parenting skills for fathers. They also offer community-service opportunities, because those activities connect inmates to important causes and show them that there are ways they can make a positive difference in this world when they get out. However, it can be hard to find a volunteer activity that fits the strict rules of the prison. No potential contraband can be a part of the volunteer experience; for example, any activity requiring scissors would be out of the question. But as it happens, counting Promise Cards meets all the standards.

Laura Miakisz is a lieutenant at the Lorain Correctional Institution. She is the one who brought *because I said I would* and this volunteering experience to the prison. Laura managed counting Promise Cards for a long time until she had to move to supervise third shift, when prisoners are sleeping. She handed over responsibility for the program to Mitchell Yancey, another officer at LCI.

As the prisoners begin their volunteer experience, a correctional officer tells them about *because I said I would* and what the Promise Cards represent. Most of them have never heard of the movement before, but it is a concept that doesn't take too much explaining. The importance of a promise is immediately relevant to many of the inmates. Many of them are struggling through issues involving self-control. Some want to commit suicide; others have intense anxiety or clinical depression as a result of being locked in a cage for the first time.

Promises written by the inmates

Every time the inmates take part in volunteer services, the facility keeps a log of their activities so that their positive contribution can be put on their permanent record. In May 2017, the logs for that month weren't done, so Laura had to sit down and watch a video recorded by the security cameras to see which inmates volunteered and for how long. She hit fast-forward so the task would go quickly. As she sat there watching the inmates work in double speed, she was fascinated by how their process would change over time. Minute by minute, she could see counting become faster. Disorganized piles would become more and more organized. The inmates have no incentive from the prison to become more productive—perhaps it is just a part of human nature that encourages us to help others. The prisoners find a sense of purpose in the work so they want to do it right.

Laura, Mitchell, and their colleagues certainly have a difficult job in the prison, working day after day with people who have committed crimes, some of which were unspeakably violent. Laura sees that many of her coworkers are pessimistic about the prospects for these inmates after they are released. "Lock them up and throw away the key" can be a somewhat common attitude. But Laura realizes that these are *people*. *People* who are going to be freed one day. They are *people* who may be your neighbor, your son's neighbor, or your grandmother's neighbor. As Laura reasons, "How we treat them is going to directly affect how they treat people later." ■

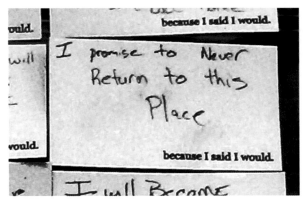

Promise Card from one of the inmates

Compassion

The World Is in Great Need

For the purposes of keeping a promise of *any* kind, self-control is the most important character value to have, and that is why it is the first element featured in this book. But it is not the most important element to *because I said I would* as a movement. The most important element to us is *compassion*.

Compassion is our number one value and the reason is simple. We are not about keeping just *any* promise. If we were, that would include the people who make terrible promises every day. You can make a promise to harm others or even yourself. It cannot be denied that there are many people in this life who are committed to tragedy and sorrow. It's not about keeping just any promise. We keep promises to eliminate suffering, build happiness, and establish peace in the world. To us, doing what is right will always be more important than keeping a promise.

There is a tremendous demand for compassion in this world, but only a limited supply. That is why you are important. It takes great strength to love those who hate, to give up something for the benefit of others, and to forgive those who have hurt you. It takes courage to be twelve-year-old Benjamin Awad and shave your head for charity knowing that some kids are going to make fun of you at school. But compassion tells Benjamin that there are some things in life more important than a bully's opinion.

Compassion takes strength, but many people mistake kindness for weakness. Some people see kindness as a type of vulnerability that is easily taken advantage of. Some people may even admire violence and anger because they represent power. But violence and anger are easy places to go. They are so simple that animals can do it. That type of aggression is just lazy. It doesn't take hard work, only thoughtless reaction. The compassionate, on the other hand, have to work much harder to mend a broken heart. If a person abuses a child in ten minutes, it may take a decade for a nonprofit to help that kid get through that experience. Compassion has a fortitude that hatred does not. *Do not take my kindness for weakness.* There is more meaning behind that phrase than many recognize.

To the *because I said I would* movement, compassion is far more than just feelings. Many people limit compassion's definition to emotions like sympathy or empathy, which are felt internally. Unfortunately, feelings and $4 will only buy you a cup of coffee. Feelings have their place, but they will not feed the homeless or clothe

the poor. Compassion is when our emotions are put into action. Compassion has to be something that is physically manifested, something that comes into the world and changes the course of events. To us, it is not compassion until something actually *happens*.

Although the battle is fought uphill, take comfort in the fact that compassion is working around the world. Contrary to the bad news that prevails on our television screens, many issues in the world are actually getting *better*. Overall, cancer death rates continue to decline among men, women, and children[4]. Over two billion people have gained access to improved drinking water since 1990[5]. Infant mortality rates in the United States have reached new all-time lows[6]. Pain exists, but the world is also seeing powerful movements where compassion is victorious. The determination of volunteers, donors, students, scientists, health-care workers, and others will not be denied.

Scientific research has also shown that compassion for others creates happiness in ourselves. Researchers in Great Britain discovered that performing daily acts of kindness for ten consecutive days results in significant boosts in happiness according to self-reported surveys. Engaging in acts of kindness causes our bodies to produce more endorphins and less of the stress hormone cortisol. Volunteers even live longer: People age fifty-five and over who volunteer for two or more organizations have 44 percent less likelihood of dying early, and that is after accounting for many other contributing factors, including gender, exercise, smoking, marital status, and many more.

Some people will never see all the benefits of compassion that

---

4   Stacy Simon, "Annual Report to the Nation: Cancer Death Rates Continue to Drop," American Cancer Society, March 31, 2017.

5   "We Can End Poverty: Millennium Development Goals and Beyond 2015," United Nations, www.un.org/millenniumgoals/environ.shtml.

6   Mark Hensch, "US Infant Mortality Rates Drop 15 Percent," The Hill, March 21, 2017, https://thehill.com/policy/healthcare/public-global-health/324960-us-infant-mortality-rates-drop-15-percent-report.

ly rightfully deserve. The world has seen many compassionate people who have been pushed around or have even died in the forts to care for those in need. The reason for compassion is no ways logical. Some people just have a hard time seeing pain an retending it doesn't exist. Maybe it is as simple as that. ■

> "One can pay back the loan of gold, but one dies forever in debt to those who are kind."
>
> —MALAYAN PROVERB

CODE OF HONOR:

Compassion

—

Through my actions, I seek to alleviate suffering, establish peace, and build happiness with others and in myself. I recognize that the world is in great need. Because of this need, I am needed. My belief in the importance of a promise is strong; however, I know that doing what is right will always be more important than keeping a promise. Commitment holds me accountable to my compassion; it does not blind me to it.

because I said I would.

STORY COLLECTION #3

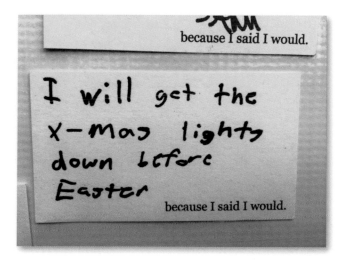

because I said I would.

I will get the X-mas lights down before Easter

because I said I would.

Love myself &
forever find my
inner beauty
because I said I would.

Jonathan and his son, Dylan

" ◄ **MY BROTHER, JONATHAN,** lived his life helping other people. He was a hard worker. His favorite thing to do was to work. His disease came out of the blue. One day when he went out to drive to work he simply couldn't start his car; his hand wouldn't work. And it was a long process to finally get his diagnosis. He had medical appointments and evaluations and exams and tests one after another, because the diagnosis is so devastating.

"In October of 2010, I was with him when he was diagnosed. The doctor told him, 'We don't know why this disease happens. We don't know why people get it. It happens to good people, hardworking people, and we must find a cure.' We knew it was Lou Gehrig's disease, that it was ALS.

"At the time, Dylan, his son, was two-and-a-half years old. Dylan knows that his dad's arms and legs stopped working. He knows that his dad couldn't eat or swallow or breath, and he knows that his dad died in February of 2013. My brother met his diagnosis with a lot of courage and bravery, and he was devoted to his son and wanted to make the most out of every moment that he could with his little boy.

"They did everything together, from watering vegetables in the garden to capturing fish in the pond behind their house to feeding the cat every morning. Dylan took care of his dad and was devoted to protecting him and making sure that he had what he needed, and his dad lived for that.

"As my brother's disease progressed, it became clear that he needed to make arrangements for his son to be cared for. And when he could still speak, my brother asked my husband and I if we would raise my nephew and take care of him when he no longer could. So I made a promise to my nephew:

'This is a promise that I am making to you that I have already made to your dad: that I will love you and raise you as my own. And I make this commitment to you as I have already made it to your father, and this is a promise that will last for the rest of your life.'"

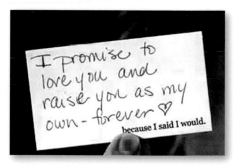

Excerpt from a video recorded with Erica

I will ask people
how they are doing
& genuinely listen.

because I said I would.

▼ **IN CLEVELAND, OHIO,** heroin and fentanyl kill more people than all homicides, suicides, and car crashes combined.[7] This epidemic does not hesitate to affect expecting mothers. Just hours old, many babies of the addicted start showing drug withdrawal symptoms, such as irritability, constant crying, joint stiffness, problems sleeping, and even seizures. The National Institute on Drug Abuse reported that, in 2012, over 21,000 babies were born suffering from opiate withdrawal—one every twenty-five minutes.[8] Many of the infants are born malnourished and struggle to keep warm.

On Saturday, May 6, 2017, the Cleveland chapter of *because I said I would* fulfilled a promise to make fleece tie blankets for babies born dependent on heroin and other opioids. Our chapter members also took the time to handwrite cards with motivational messages for the mothers who are fighting hard to recover and become sober. Many judge these mothers for what they have done to their babies, but no guilt is stronger than the sense of shame they put on themselves. Although blankets and notes provide only a small step in helping address this horrific problem that Cuyahoga County faces, doing something is certainly better than doing nothing.

7   David Petkiewics, "Heroin and fentanyl killed more people in Cuyahoga County in 2016 than homicides, suicides, and car crashes," Cleveland.com, June 05, 2017, http://www.cleveland.com/metro/index.ssf/2017/05/heroin_and_fentanyl_killed_mor.html.

8   "Dramatic Increases in Maternal Opioid Use and Neonatal Abstinence Syndrome," National Institute on Drug Use, September 2015, https://www.drugabuse.gov/related-topics/trends-statistics/infographics/dramatic-increases-in-maternal-opioid-use-neonatal-abstinence-syndrome.

◀CHAPTER MEMBERS of *because I said I would* keep their promise to donate blood together. One pint of blood can save as many as three lives.

I promise to promote water safety education to save lives! To start a foundation in memory of Matt!

because I said I would.

I will visit WILL
for his 40th
BIRTHday !

because I said I would.

▲ Family exercise time

▲*BECAUSE I SAID I WOULD* **MEMBERS** work through personal development workshops at our monthly meet ups. We learn a new concept each month that helps us get better at keeping our personal promises. Whether it's about time management, controlling our word choice, the fallibility of human memory, or other topics, we try to build our personal development workshops on the foundation of scientific research. Inspiring words can only take you so far. We need research and evidence-based practices to take us the rest of the way.

I NOTICE WHEN girls have tan lines from their sports bras, and instantly find connections through that," says Anne.

Anne started running for perhaps a different reason than most. She was looking for a way to stay busy and maybe make some new friends. Her husband was deployed in the navy for a year on a submarine, and she was living in a new town. Anne certainly stays connected with her husband during deployments, but little things can change over that much time. As she puts it, "He came home to a running wife."

"I was finally able to share my 2016 medal collection with him. It was my first year as a runner and my first year completing a New Year's resolution. In 2016, I lived life because I said I would. I ran. I completed three half marathons. I didn't always stick to my training plan, but always finished the race," she told me.

Anne had a display rack custom-made for her medals. She s proud that her accomplishments have helped support charity races around the country. In fact, she often donates her medals to a nonprofit that gives them to patients in the hospital who could use some encouragement in hard times. Anne includes a handwritten note with hers.

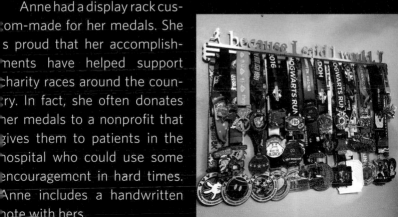

▲ This is Miska. He is our Cofounder's dog. Why put him in the book? Because he's a good boy. Aren't you, Miska? Yes, you are.

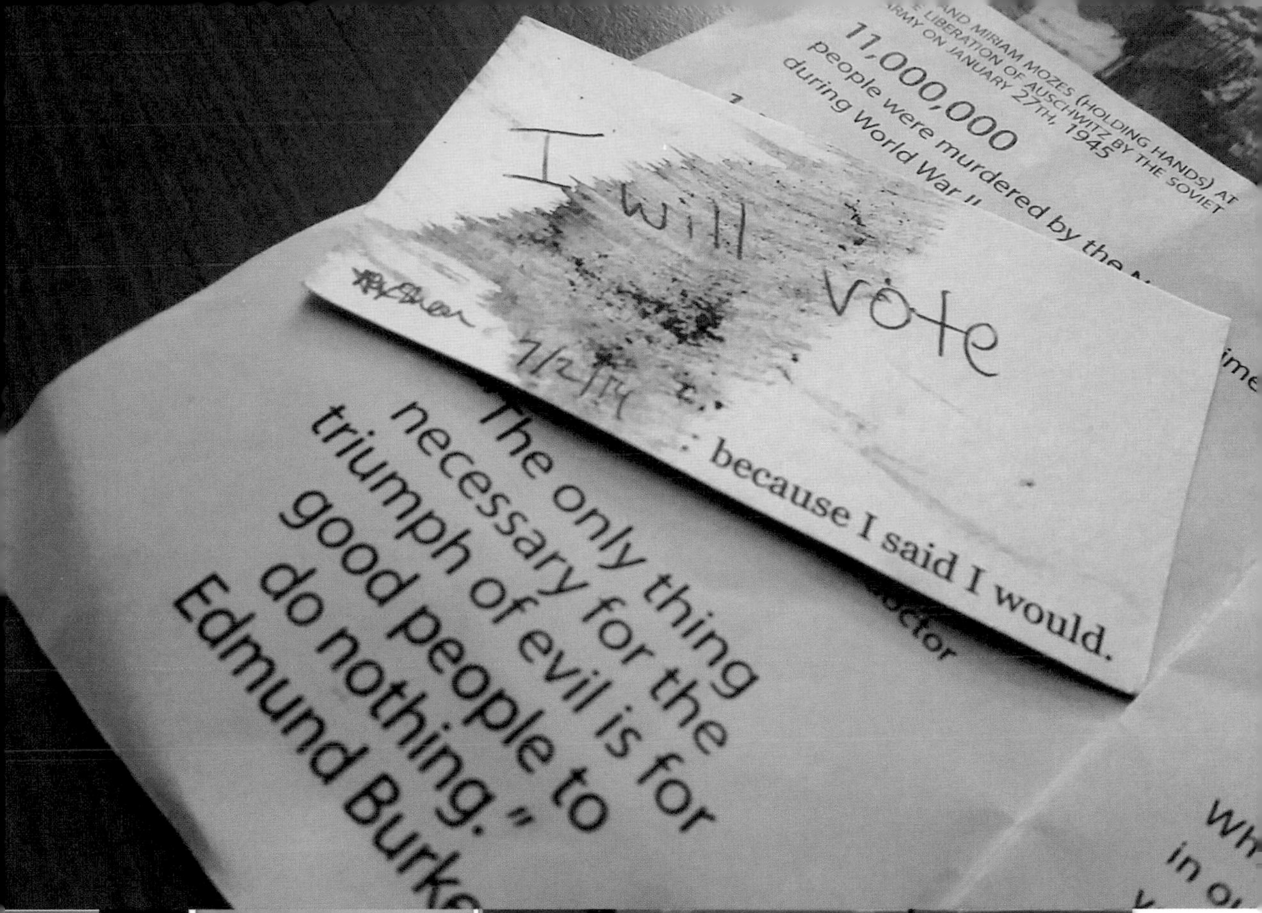

I will vote

because I said I would.

"The only thing necessary for the triumph of evil is for good people to do nothing."
Edmund Burke

11,000,000 people were murdered by the N... during World War II

...AND MIRIAM MOZES (HOLDING HANDS) AT ... THE LIBERATION OF AUSCHWITZ BY THE SOVIET ARMY ON JANUARY 27TH, 1945

LAKEWOOD
02-I

because I said I would.

One Day It Will Be Too Late

Amber and Her Kidney

In December 2014, Amber was scrolling through Facebook when she came across a picture that was shared by the martial arts school her daughter attended. The picture was from a crowdfunding project that looked interesting, so she clicked. Amber described the photo to me on the phone. "It was a man and a woman and they were holding this half billboard-type sign. It said *Dad of six* and all of their kids were in front of them."

In this picture, this couple's oldest son was over six feet tall and their youngest child was only eighteen months old. The father's name was Darin, and he needed a kidney or he would die.

Amber

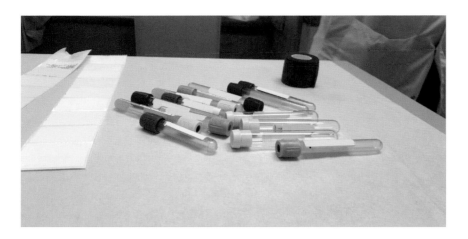

Amber said, "The page had all sorts of information about his life, his children, his blood type and the blood types he could accept, and information about how to get tested to see if you were a match. I decided, 'Hey, why not at least see. It's a very simple blood test.'"

One click led to another. And another. And another. Amber came across a phone number. She called it and made an appointment to get her blood drawn. The visit to the hospital was quick. To call it a procedure would be an exaggeration. It was a little prick, and within a couple minutes, the nurse had what she needed to send to the lab.

About two weeks later, Amber was at work when her cell phone rang. The caller informed Amber that she was the best potential match for Darin. The next stage of testing needed to start soon.

"I reached out to Darin's family, thinking that would give me some sort of accountability," Amber recalls. "I even remember messaging his wife something to the effect of *The only way this isn't going to happen is if something is medically wrong with me*. That's when I really started doing the research. It all seemed like a hypothetical scenario until this point."

The research taught Amber that being a hero takes a lot more than just saying a comforting promise to someone who needs to hear it.

The second stage of testing cannot be compared to the first. It was far from a quick visit. The hospital assigned Amber a caseworker. Psychological evaluations were necessary to determine if her state of mind was fit for the operation. Then more medical testing. She needed to find a caretaker who would look after her and her daughter during the long weeks of recovery. Even with an incredible likelihood of survival, she still needed to have discussions with her family members about what to do if things went wrong during surgery.

"That's when things went downhill," Amber says. "Nobody was supportive. Nobody said they would watch my dogs. Nobody said they would help me take care of my kid." Before you judge Amber's friends and family, realize that Amber was dear to them, and Darin was a stranger. Whatever they could do to put up a barrier, they felt they had to try. In their minds, they were protecting her.

"Evidently, I wasn't that strong at that point in time because I let all of those people frighten me." Amber became convinced that this genuinely wasn't her problem. This was a stranger to which she had no obligation.

Within a few weeks of Amber's first appointment, she pulled out, and the hospital informed Darin and his family that the donor was no longer interested.

Amber's life went on. She told me on the phone that, in complete honesty, she didn't think about Darin for an entire year. Amber explained that she is very confident that she didn't think about him because if she were to have really thought things over, it would have eaten her alive. She was free from those thoughts . . . until one day when Darin appeared on the news.

"Yellow. That's what he looked like. He looked like he was dying," Amber remembered later.

There had been no other match, and time was running out. There are very few moments in life when our regret and guilt is so *undeniable*—when we don't have to carry the weight of our own mistakes, but instead, that weight is carried by someone else. Someone else's husband. Someone else's father. Staring into that screen, Amber couldn't take it anymore.

"I immediately reached out without hesitation. When I realized Darin wasn't going to make it was the exact moment I decided I would be his donor. And I remember telling my mother, 'I don't care if I have to hire somebody to be my caretaker. I'm doing it. If you won't do it, I will find somebody, even if I have to spend money to do it. I will find somebody that will support me.'

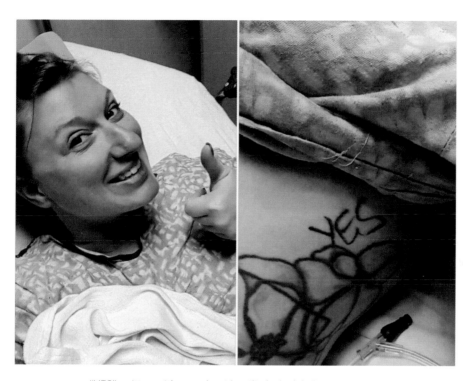

"YES" written with a marker identified which kidney to remove

"I decided that it *was* my problem, and I immediately regretted backing out. Knowing that he could have had all that time over that past year back with his kids was heartrending. Testing took two full days. CT scans, PET scans, blood work, psych screenings, and meetings with social workers and surgeons and dozens of other people—and each one of them told me, 'You can back out at any time.'"

There would be no more broken promises in this story, though. On April 18, 2016, Amber's left kidney, the strongest of her two, was removed from her body and donated to a father who would get a chance to see his children grow up.

Today, Amber is a fierce advocate of organ donation. She has even given presentations on the subject of electing to have your organs donated after you die. Amber speaks about the decision in very blunt terms: "You don't need them, and someone else does."

Right now as you read this, more than 100,000 people in the United States are awaiting kidney transplants, according to figures from the National Kidney Foundation. In 2014, 4,761 patients died while waiting for a kidney transplant, while another 3,668 people became too sick to receive a kidney transplant.[9]

Amber made a dishonorable decision when she first turned her back on the promise she made to a wife in crisis. But just because the errors of our ways exist does not mean they need to persist. Go back. Turn around and face what you know is right, even if it ends up being too late. The chance may still be there to correct your mistake, but for how long? ■

Amber at the hospital after donating her kidney

9   "Organ Donation and Transplant Statistics," National Kidney Foundation, Accessed on May 03, 2018. http://www.easybib.com/guides/citation-guides/chicago-turabian/how-to-cite-a-website-chicago-turabian/.

Bags on the Porch

Rachael's Favorite Holiday

Rachael Awad lives in a small town in Fresno County, California. One morning, she was watching the morning news with her two kids, Ben (eight) and Jasmine (nine). Rachael has been doing this since they were very young because she wants them to understand what is happening in the world.

On this mid-September morning, as the local news played on the TV in the background, Rachael talked with her kids about Halloween, which was only six weeks away—and Rachael's favorite holiday. Every year, she plans the family's costumes weeks in advance, decorates their

house inside and out, and hosts a big party. As they were chatting about their plans, a segment on the local news talked about a nonprofit organization that shelters adults and children affected by domestic violence. The organization was called the Marjaree Mason Center, and they strive to end the cycle of abuse through education and advocacy. According to the National Coalition Against Domestic Violence, nearly twenty people per minute are physically abused by an intimate partner in the United States.[10] That's more than ten million women and men a year.

---

10 Black, M.C., Basile, K.C., Breiding, M.J., Smith, S.G., Walters, M.L., Merrick, M.T., Chen, J., and Stevens, M.R. "The National Intimate Partner and Sexual Violence Survey (NISVS): 2010 Summary Report," Atlanta, GA: National Center for Injury Prevention and Control, Centers for Disease Control and Prevention, 2011, https://www.cdc.gov/violenceprevention/pdf/nisvs_report2010-a.pdf.

As Rachael listened to this segment, something occurred to her about the upcoming holiday: *The children staying in those safe houses probably don't have Halloween costumes.*

To Rachael, Halloween without a costume is an abomination, so she started posting on Facebook, asking people for costumes they no longer wanted. But with the holiday coming up soon, unfortunately, many families did not have spares to donate. To get all the children in the shelter a costume, Rachael would have to go out and buy them herself. She combed through discount stores and thrift shops, looking for anything she could afford. That first year, Rachael donated more than fifty costumes.

"So the second year, I was a little more prepared for what I was walking into," Rachael told me. "I started reaching out to the kids' schools right after Halloween the first year." Rachael figured that kids grow out of their mermaid tails and superhero spandex pretty quickly, and so right after Halloween more families would be open to donating them. And that is exactly what happened. Rachael was able to get a lot of gently used Halloween cos-

Rachael's kids

tumes. With her novice sewing skills, she repaired tears and split seams, fixing up the ones that needed a little attention.

By the time the third Halloween came around, random strangers started dropping off costumes at her house. She would pull up to her driveway and see a bunch of bulging plastic bags sitting on her porch, knowing exactly what they were. She had become known as the "Halloween Lady," which sounds kind of creepy but is totally not in this particular case.

2018 is Rachael's seventh year of donating costumes. Her last round included more

Bags of donated costumes

than 280 donated outfits. This is not an official nonprofit organization. This is a woman with a pickup truck who keeps her promises. Rachael has even held an unofficial *because I said I would* assembly at her local elementary school, where she distributes thousands of Promise Cards, encouraging the students to make positive commitments like her own.

For so many causes in need, we'd like to believe that the cavalry is on its way. There is a volunteer, a donor, or organization willing to help these people, right? No, it doesn't always work out like that. If not for Rachael Awad, those kids wouldn't have costumes. They wouldn't get that happy Halloween memory. If not for Rachael, the school assembly wouldn't happen and the Promise Cards would never get written by those children. There is only one Halloween Lady in her town. Rachael's promise to children affected by domestic violence reminds me of a thought that often rattles in my head: *If I don't do it, no one else will.*

That might sound like a pessimistic view of society, but I believe it is really more of a statement of how powerful a single person can be. ■

Halloween costume donations from sixth year of Rachael's efforts

The Chief Volunteer

Pat Visits on Wednesday

Pat Bakos is a retiree who lives near the *because I said I would* head-quarters in the Cleveland area. For fifteen years of her career, Pat worked at *The Plain Dealer*, which is the strange name of our city's largest newspaper. Interestingly enough, Pat found out about us through the same medium. A local newspaper ran an article that mentioned we were in desperate need of volunteers to count Promise Cards. Pat saw the call to action and came in one day to help out.

Counting Promise Cards is a curious activity. And by *curious*, I mean super boring. It is literally just counting to ten over and over and over again, but I guess it does allow you to take your mind off things for a while. The real entertainment in this type of volunteering actually comes from the conversations you have with other volunteers while your hands continue working on autopilot.

Pat soon became a regular volunteer with us, and she is as reliable as the sunrise, so we made her our chief volunteer. Pat leads a group from the Cuyahoga County Board of Developmental Disabilities while they visit our facility every Wednesday.

Promise Card mailings

This is a program provided by the county that helps individuals with developmental disabilities gain more independence by connecting them with paying jobs at companies. These individuals go to work as a group, which helps keep things organized for their special needs. Several of these employees decided that they wanted to give back to others by volunteering with our nonprofit.

Volunteers are sometimes hard to come by, and the support of this group makes a huge difference. How huge? Well over 100,000 Promise Cards have been counted or mailed by these giving souls.

Pat supports this team on their visits to the office. She even engineered an ingenious placemat for a few of the volunteers who struggle with counting. The placemat has ten designated spots, one for each card. All you have to do is fill up the rectangle boxes with Promise Cards, and they know the stack is accurate. Because of Pat's leadership with this group, *because I said I would* received the 2016 Inclusion Award from the Cuyahoga County Board of Developmental Disabilities.

I once asked Pat why she cares so much about promises. She simply said, "It is something you can do when you are very young until your last day." Pat keeps her promises to volunteer at *because I said I would*, but she also delivers food to seniors through Meals on Wheels and volunteers at

Seeds of Literacy, another nonprofit in Cleveland. Pat is spending her retirement as a model citizen.

You might assume that Pat has volunteered at places throughout her life. That's what I assumed for years, but I was corrected recently. In the conversation we had about including her in the book, she told me that counting Promise Cards with *because I said I would* at age seventy-one was her first time volunteering. That just goes to show that it's never too late to start. If you haven't tried volunteering, you should. According to the Bureau of Labor Statistics, 75.1 percent of Americans do not volunteer even one hour in an entire year.[11] It's not that we all have to be a bunch of Pats. But if we all volunteered a couple hours here and there, it would add up pretty quickly. ■

11   "Volunteering in the United States," Bureau of Labor Statistics, February 25, 2016. https://www.bls.gov/news.release/volun.nr0.htm.

Ten-Minute Walk

A Fall Night after a Football Game

From time to time, a supporter will personally hand me a promise they have made and ask me to hold on to it until the promise is kept. Yet among all the Promise Cards I have ever held, I have never seen a promise quite like the one in this story. I told the young woman who handed me this card that I would return it to her should she honor her word.

The girl who wrote this card has asked to remain nameless. That wish will be respected. These are photos from a scrapbook that symbolize her story. These are her words:

> I grew up in a really great family, in a nice town. I was pretty outgoing and talkative as a little kid. My parents were won-derful and supportive. They raised me to be strong and always

encouraged me to explore and try new things. My family was really close during my childhood. We even had a family game night almost every week.

I tried just about every sporting activity you can imagine during elementary and middle school. Soccer, tee ball, dancing, swimming, figure skating. It was dancing and figure skating that I loved the most, and I stuck with them both through high school.

Like most teenagers, that's when I started dating. I was fifteen when I met a boy who would change my life forever. He was from a neighboring school; he was cute, and so sweet to me. We started dating a few weeks before homecoming weekend. We settled on an agreement. We would go to his high school's homecoming football game, and he would come to my high school's homecoming dance.

I was pretty excited the night of the game. The weather was beautiful, and the game was great. His school's team won. I even got to meet some of the little kids he coached in football. During that game, I grew to like him even more. The game ended, and we decided to walk back to his house. It was only a ten-minute walk from the high school.

We were about a block from his home when he asked if I

would sit with him and look at the stars for a few minutes. I had told him during one of our first conversations that I loved looking at the stars. It was cute that he had asked. It was such a romantic gesture, and I was surprised he even remembered, so we sat down in the grass in a neighbor's side yard a block from his house.

Unfortunately, that is where my life would change forever. In that yard, under that sky, he pinned me down. I struggled. He was not the boy who I thought he was. I wanted to scream, but nothing came out. He raped me.

After this happened, everything in my life was separated into two parts: before and after. I couldn't bring myself to tell my parents about what he had done to me. A lot of people experience posttraumatic stress disorder after a violent sexual assault. For me, that meant every night, a vivid nightmare would play where dreams once were. A moment you want to forget forever now becomes a flash back during class, lunch at school, or at the dinner table with your family—over and over again.

I started to skip school more than I went. The once outgoing part of me became shy and quiet. I began to self-harm. Eventually, the school intervened because I was disrupting class by leaving in the middle of lessons because I was crying. The school counselor recommended to my parents that I enter an outpatient mental health program. They still didn't know what had happened, what he had done to me, but later that night, I broke down and told them. It's a hard thing to say out loud, but with those words, I was finally able to breathe again. I didn't have to bear that weight alone anymore. After some time had passed, I told myself it was too late to tell the police, that I should try to forget it, but in counseling, I learned that this isn't something that can just be forgotten.

One day, I promised that I would testify. I promised to prosecute, and I did. He was sentenced. The truth is, though, that this story isn't about me. It isn't about the person who harmed me, either. I testified against my rapist because of a complete stranger—a person who, in fact, I will never meet.

Let me explain. You see, someone who is willing to violently abuse another human being, well . . . they might do it again, and again, and again. I testified against my rapist to protect a stranger, someone who will never have to know the pain that I have been through because the man who is going to assault them is in prison now. He's going to think twice before ever doing what he did to me to someone else.

Perpetrators need to know that prosecution looms over their shoulders. Survivors, we need to find the courage to prosecute. We cannot change what happened to us, but we can control whether or not we choose to fight back. You may think it's too late, but it's not. It's never too late to take a stand. It was a difficult time for me, but you know what? I don't care. I would prosecute again in a heartbeat. I will not stand idle. I will not let this happen without consequence. This isn't justice; it's protection. The thought that maybe some young girl out there sleeps better tonight because I scraped together enough courage to stand trial, because I fought so she wouldn't have to . . . . This story isn't about me.

My rape doesn't define me. I'm defined by my actions. I define myself by the good I bring into this world, not by the good that was taken from me. I testified against my rapist *because I said I would*.

The court date was pushed back, but the promise was kept. I mailed this card back to its rightful owner.

The witness stand is a hard place to be for a rape victim. Your character is questioned. Implications are made. But at some moment, sitting in that chair, you remember that what has happened to you is over. It is now time to protect a stranger you will never meet—a person who will never feel your pain, because the person who would have hurt them is now in prison. ∎

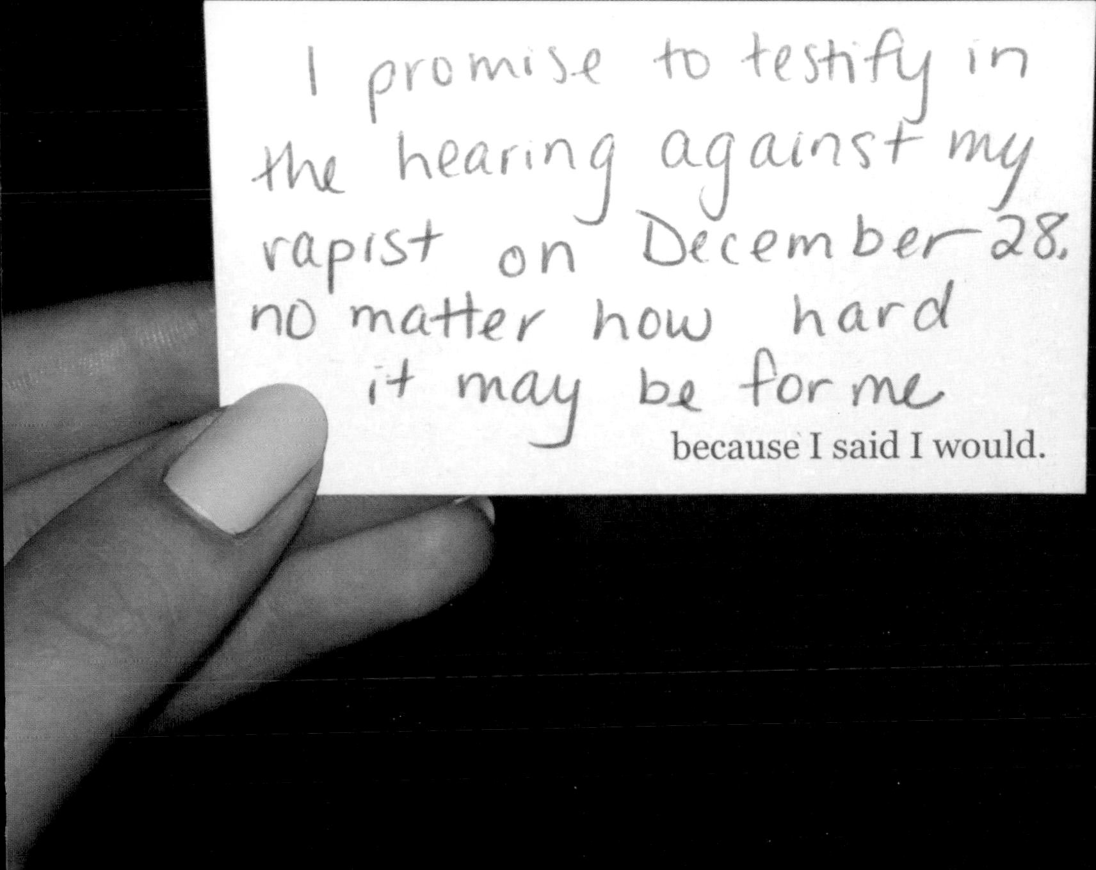
I promise to testify in the hearing against my rapist on December 28. no matter how hard it may be for me
because I said I would.

Contemplation

PLANNING AND CAREFUL CONSIDERATION

1. Self-Control
2. Compassion
3. **Contemplation**
4. Honesty
5. Accountability
6. Sacrifice
7. Hope

Motivation is essential to keeping promises, but it is easily overvalued. Everyone likes to feel excited and excitement makes for easier work, but all of this energy has its limits. There are some obstacles that motivation cannot change and only careful planning can overcome. Take Rachael Awad, for example. She started collecting Halloween costumes for children affected by domestic violence *almost a year in advance* because she knew that right after Halloween is when families donate their outfits. Miss the timing, miss the costumes. Or there's Moira McGovern and her promise to lose fifty pounds in order to skydive with her nephew. Clearly, that weight couldn't be lost in a day. Her fitness plan required time and support.

Plans should *precede* promises. Unfortunately, that's not how many people operate. People often jump to a commitment by communicating their promise first, leaving planning as an afterthought. Maybe you have accidentally found yourself in this situation. You quickly say yes to a commitment and your very next thought sounds something like . . .

Wait . . . Am I available on that day?
Umm . . . Do I have enough money to do that?
Uhhh . . . How much time is that actually going to take?

We need to plan *then* promise, not the other way around. It's about measuring feasibility. Why would you commit to something that you aren't sure is even feasible? There is often an exhaustive list of traps and hurdles that get in the way of our best intentions: weather, traffic, funding, equipment failure, our physical ability, our level of motivation, other decision makers, or third parties, to name a few. The list goes on. Account for these variables first and shape your promise around the limitations they create. If you are suddenly asked for a commitment without enough time to think it through, ask for a pause. Tell the person that you respect them too much to make a promise to them that you aren't sure you can keep. Ask for some time to think it over.

It is often said, "If you really care about something, you'll make the time." This phrase irritates me, because *time cannot be made.* Time can only be accounted for and reserved. It may seem that I am being a bit too literal with my interpretation of this saying, but perhaps you have noticed people in your life who are truly acting as if time can be made from nothing. They leave their house late and somehow they are surprised they don't arrive on time, as if driving doesn't take time and traffic isn't a thing.

We call this poor *time consciousness.* Time consciousness is one's awareness of the current time and how it relates to the sequence of events necessary to accomplish a task or project. Here are a few ways you can spot a person with good time consciousness:

- They tell you they are going to miss a deadline five days in advance, not a half hour before.

- They aren't shy about ending a conversation quickly because they know they need to leave soon to stay on schedule.

- They are more concerned than the average person about things they have never done before because they don't know how much time to estimate for those tasks.

- They check their watch and their calendar consistently during the day and before making promises.

There are a few ways to build stronger time consciousness, and detailed calendaring is probably the best one of them. For those who are elite with their promises, it is not uncommon to see ten to twenty items on their calendar in a given day. They don't just calendar physical meetings with other people. They calendar independent tasks, routine chores, and mundane responsibilities because they want to have a full comprehension of their capacity, not just a grasp of meetings with other people. Disciplined calendaring practices can help us identify conflicts, calculate timelines, discover hidden challenges, and build time consciousness that can serve all promises. Employing a checklist is a close relative of calendaring. Front-loading your worries and concerns onto a checklist can also prevent errors that happen when things start moving fast. Take the airline industry as an example. A commercial flight has not crashed and resulted in a fatality in the United States since 2009.[12] That's over 800 million passengers and not a single death, according to the US Department of Transportation.[13] This is because airlines have turned their contemplation into a checklist, and pilots live in a culture that respects checklists as imperative tools, not bureaucracy. Human memory has its limits. It is inevitable that we will forget a little task or small piece of equipment. This is where promises start to break down.

If it sounds like meticulous calendaring and exhaustive checklists are really boring, that's because they are. A lot of people won't take the time to carefully calendar, but a lot of people don't keep promises either.

Many people assume these detailed tactics add stress to life, but there is evidence that the opposite might be true. When stress levels of 249 students at a Midwestern university were assessed, researchers found that one of the most successful techniques for controlling stress was effective time management.[14] It rated *above* all other strategies, including avoidance, social support, fitness activities, and

12   David Shepardson, "2017 safest year on record for commercial passenger air travel: groups," Reuters, January 1, 2018, https://www.reuters.com/article/us-aviation-safety/2017-safest-year-on-record-for-commercial-passenger-air-travel-groups-idUSKBN1EQ17L.

13   "Beyond Traffic 2045 Trends and Choices," U.S Department of Transportation, p238. Accessed on May 3, 2018, https://cms.dot.gov/sites/dot.gov/files/docs/Draft_Beyond_Traffic_Framework.pdf.

14   Ranjita Misra and Michelle McKean, "College students' academic stress and its relation to their anxiety, time management, and leisure satisfaction," *American Journal of Health Studies*, 16:1, 41-51, 2000, https://search.proquest.com/openview/c2c1309ac42c1cc4h74e146f6b0e26 0c/1?pq-origsite=gscholar&cbl=30166.

leisure pursuits. Why is that? A lot of the time, we are worrying because there is no plan.

Am I going to have enough time to get that done?

Are there any supplies I forgot to order?

Oh no, I forgot to do something. I don't have enough time now!

Take your worries and imprison them on a calendar and or a checklist. If you can do that consistently, you may increase your ability to live in the moment. When a worry arises, you can say to yourself:

That's already accounted for on my calendar.

There's a time and place to worry about that, and that time isn't right now.

I am where I am supposed to be. I am doing what I am supposed to be doing.

Because I said I would has developed a Promise Planner™ template that you can use to help you contemplate your promises. Our local chapters, our character education programming with students, and our employees all use the Promise Planner to help with contemplation. Perhaps fittingly, it's sort of a checklist in itself. It challenges you to think of possible barriers to success and provides some best practices that your promises might need. Our hope is that the Promise Planner is reasonably simple and self-explanatory. Fill it out using one of your promises, and its functionality and benefits should become much clearer than just the blank form. If you need a downloadable and printable copy at no cost, simply visit becauseisaidiwould.com/promiseplanner. We just ask that this tool not be used for commercial purposes.

Planning is only the first of two parts that make up *because I said I would*'s view of contemplation. The second part is about thinking through cause and effect. We must work to ensure that our promises actually accomplish their intent. That might sound obvious at first, but many endeavors fall short of this goal on accident because the cause and effect of the promises have not been well researched or measured.

Name:

Promise Planner

Draft word choice for your promise:

I will...

┌─────────────────────────────────┐
│   │
│   │
│   FINAL WRITTEN PROMISE   │
│   CARD GOES HERE.   │
│   │
│   │
because I said I would. │   │
└─────────────────────────────────┘

Start date: _____ / _____ / 20___
Month   Day   Year

Completion date: _____ / _____ / 20___
Month   Day   Year

Other parties involved:

Name:_____

Name:_____

Name:_____

Name:_____

Possible barriers to success:

Yes No
☐ ☐ Knowledge / talent / experience

☐ ☐ External party cooperation

☐ ☐ Personal learning curves / possible mistakes

☐ ☐ Traffic / transportation / weather

☐ ☐ Loss of motivation

Yes No
☐ ☐ Forgetfulness

☐ ☐ Resources / funding

☐ ☐ Equipment / supplies failure

☐ ☐ Lack of adequate time / poor time estimates

☐ ☐ Arising priorities or conflicting emergencies

☐ ☐ Other(s) _____

I commit to these best practices:

Yes No
☐ ☐ Calendaring tasks

☐ ☐ Accountability partner(s): _____

☐ ☐ Checklist(s)

Yes No
☐ ☐ Written communication with all parties

☐ ☐ Back up plan(s)

☐ ☐ Motivators:_____

Actionable steps (check as completed):

☐ 1. _____

☐ 2. _____

☐ 3. _____

☐ 4. _____

☐ 5. _____

☐ Completed   ☐ Qualifies for Achievement Badge

Let's use Scared Straight programs as an example. Scared Straight programs put at-risk youth through fearful experiences in adult prisons. The intent is to deter the kids from choosing a life of crime by showing them the harsh realities of adult prison life. This approach was studied by Campbell Collaboration, a nonprofit that researches social, behavioral, and educational programs, and they discovered that Scared Straight programs actually increase criminal activity in youth by 28 percent compared to nonparticipants.[15] The program accomplishes the *opposite* of its well-meaning intent to such an extent that the United States Department of Justice has made a very strong official statement saying that these types of programs should never be used.[16]

Humanitarianism, personal development, community action—these are not surface-level endeavors. The stakes are high and it is essential that we work to understand the true cause and effect of our actions.

We only have a finite time on this earth. How are you going to spend yours? We don't want to answer that question for you, but we do beg you to ask it of yourself. Contemplate. Our lives are run by unspoken expectations and well-established cultural norms that may or may not be good for humanity. Plato once said, "An unexamined life is not worth living." I cannot fully agree with that quote, but I understand at least a part of its meaning. ■

15   Petrosino A, Turpin-Petrosino C, Hollis-Peel M, and Julia Lavenberg, "Scared Straight and Other Juvenile Awareness Programs for Preventing Juvenile Delinquency: A Systematic Review," Campbell Systematic Reviews, June, 2012, https://www.campbellcollaboration.org/media/k2/attachments/Petrosino_Scared_Straight_Update.pdf.

16   "Scared Straight: Don't Believe the Hype," Coalition for Juvenile Justice, Accessed on May 3, 2018, http://juvjustice.org/sites/default/files/resource-files/resource_539_0.pdf.

Contemplation

—

I reserve time to understand the world and attempt to understand my place in it. When I see that my commitment is needed, I remember that promises are not easy to keep. I believe in planning and careful consideration. My words and actions have consequences. I should be patient with both.

because I said I would.

because I said I would.

Create **LASTIN** change <u></u>

beca

id I would.

◄ A college philanthropy club squad pic

Remove myself from technology to focus on family time for a minimum of 1HR Daily. because I said I would.

Even puppies deserve promises.

▲ **IN DECEMBER 2016,** a lot of political news channels were angry with debate regarding refugees coming into the United States. As a nonpartisan nonprofit, we try to stay out of political rhetoric. There are many issues in the center of the political spectrum that people from nearly all walks of life can agree with, and this movement tries to keep its focus there. However, when it comes to refugees, we have no problem drawing the line. There are fewer things more humanitarian than sheltering and shielding the persecuted. One of *because I said I would's* supporters, Eva Kor, survived the Holocaust, and we will not let those lessons of history be forgotten.

On Saturday, December 10, 2016, the Cleveland chapter of *because I said I would* fulfilled a promise to welcome refugees to our country and help them make a connection to their new home. We threw a bowling party for them because we thought that sounded super American. We even invited a local legend, Adam Barta, who is the *Guinness World Record* holder for "Highest Pinfall in Tenpin Bowling in 1 Hour by an Individual." The party was a huge success, with forty chapter members and a hundred refugees in attendance!

I will eat to life and not live to eat.

because I said I would.

Malik,
    I will pay for your
'Pay to Play' sports programs
at Westerville North.
    Love, Grandma
                    because I said I would.

I will make my
father proud and
go to college.

~~[scribbled out]~~.

because I said I would.

▲ **IN LATE 2017,** we launched *because I said I would* high school chapters. Following in the path of our city-based adult chapters, these student members keep promises to help people in need and become better citizens through personal development workshops. We hope to start a thousand high school chapters one day, along with chapters at colleges, middle schools, and elementary schools. As I write this, we only have three high school chapters, but you've got to start somewhere.

Eight Hundred and Twenty-Six

Garth's Promise to Emma

G arth Callaghan is forty-eight years old and lives in a quaint town just north of Richmond, Virginia. Garth is what you might call a "cheesy dad"—the kind of dad whose jokes are so *not* funny that they somehow go full circle to being funny again. For example, I bet he loves this one:

Why do chicken coops only have two doors?
Because if they had four doors, they would be chicken sedans!

Garth is also a bit nerdy for *Star Wars*. He owns fifty-five different *Star Wars* shirts. Fifty-five is not a number I just made up. It's the exact number he told me to include in this story. Every day, Garth is searching for an excuse to dress up as a Jedi Knight. (That might be a bit of an exaggeration, but also maybe not.)

Even with all his geekiness, Garth's wife, Lissa, and his only child, Emma, love him very much. He tries hard to be a good parent, and that can be seen in Emma's lunchbox every day. Every day since the second grade, Emma has received little napkin notes from her dad tucked in with her packed meal. You know the kind of thing I'm talking about—words of love and encouragement scribbled on a paper napkin. That may seem sweet and adorable at first, but imagine you're an eight-year-old girl in the cafeteria, and as you are chewing into your PB&J you read, *Remember that guy who quit? NEITHER DOES ANYONE ELSE.*

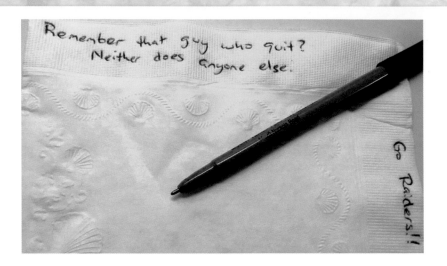

Apparently, Garth believes that bench-pressing motivational quotes pair well with wheat bread.

In fairness to Garth, though, let's imagine his situation for a moment. This guy has to go to work. He's the sole breadwinner. He's got to take care of his family, the finances, and a bunch of other adult stuff.

While he is busy doing that, his daughter is growing up. Time waits for no one. One day, Emma is in the second grade, and then before you know it, she is in the eighth grade. She has sports practice, homework, and friends. Overlap their schedules and you see there's not much overlap at all. How much *quality time* does Garth get to spend with Emma? Maybe it's an hour a day—that's sixty minutes to take the most precious thing in your existence, your baby girl, and build her into a woman of character. It's not so easy.

So, yes, the notes are cheesy, but the guy is doing his best. And as the years go by, these little scribbles come to mean a lot to Emma. Even if her dad can be embarrassing at times, these notes show that he cares.

> Dear Emma,
> You believed in Santa for all those years. You can believe in yourself for 5 minutes.
>
> Love, Dad
> PS - I believe in you all of the time!

Now, my own father never wrote me any napkin notes, and that is quite all right. Every dad does his job differently.

But unfortunately, there is something else that Emma's father and my father do have in common. Garth was also diagnosed with stage IV cancer, but it's in his kidney. This is not the kind you can just cut out. It's the kind that makes you write advanced medical directives. It's the kind that necessitates a last will and testament. In 2013, Garth was told that he had an 8 percent chance of living past five years.

When someone tells you that the ride is almost over, that your time on this earth is coming to a close, you begin to reflect on the concept of time and how you spend it. You consider what you are truly committed to. You think about everybody that you love. Those are the thoughts that coursed through Garth's mind.

> Dear Emma,
> Sometimes when I need a miracle, I look in to your eyes and realize I've already created one.
>
> Love, Dad

As his diagnosis sunk in, Garth thought about Emma. Then a thought came to him. Garth began gathering a bunch of calendars for the coming years. He needed them to make a specific calculation. When he was finished, he searched through his belongings for a Promise Card and wrote . . .

Eight hundred and twenty-six is the exact number of days Emma has left until she graduates from high school, and that's how many napkin notes Garth began writing that day. No matter what happens to him, no matter what day is their last goodbye, even if he cannot be there for her, those napkin notes will be. Every single one has been written in advance.

This, to me, isn't a story about a good father. In fact, maybe your dad was never there for you. This isn't a story about cancer either, although

I hope this disease never crosses your path. No, this is about *doing what you can with what you've got*. Life is not fair, and unfortunately it never will be. Sometimes, we have to stop worrying about what could have been and start doing what's possible right now. We have to take what little we are given and make the best of it. Even if the days are numbered.

2018 is Emma's senior year at Hermitage High School. Since 2013, her father has received chemotherapy on a daily basis, but he is still fighting. Garth has lost fifty-five pounds since the beginning of his treatment. Garth still has cancer, but at least it is not growing. Experimental treatments have left him fatigued and depleted.

"I am less capable of being a dad and a husband," he says. "It is robbing my wife and my daughter. I feel less. Less alive than I want to be."

Garth believes he has done what he can for his little girl. As Emma nears graduation, Garth's attention turns to his wife, Lissa. Lissa has been out of the workforce for twenty years because her job was to take care of the family. "Now I need to make sure Lissa doesn't become lost," Garth says. ■

Emma's high school senior picture

Covered in Bumper Stickers

Laurie Deserves a Vacation

In our weekly staff meetings, all *because I said I would* employees write individual Promise Cards, usually about something personal. It's a small action we take to try to walk the walk. But on August 6, 2016, Laurie Wise-Maher, our vice president of development at the time, was feeling ready to put commitment on hold for a while. She was about to go on a much-deserved vacation—an eight-day camping trip splitting time between Letchworth State Park in New York and Cook Forest State Park in Pennsylvania. The day before she left for this trip, Laurie and I were looking at buying a funeral home for the organization. I understand

how weird that sounds, but hear me out. Our nonprofit was growing, and we needed more office space. We wanted to stop throwing money away on rent, and this particular funeral home was up for sale and incredibly affordable. We thought it wouldn't hurt to at least take a look. After all, the place was modern, updated, and not at all creepy.

Just kidding. It was totally creepy in a Scooby-Doo kind of way. The building dated from before the turn of the twentieth century, and the people who built it probably had friends fighting in the Civil War at the time. The basement had a huge hole in the floorboards where I am assuming all the demons lived.

After taking a walk through this funeral home, Laurie and I sat on the porch stairs of the building and talked. While there were some plus sides to the place, we both agreed that it wasn't for us. We didn't want to answer the question "Didn't this used to be a funeral home?" twenty times a day, and our office dog is afraid of ghosts. With the decision mutually made, Laurie gave me a hug and got into her Honda Element to start her vacation.

Laurie's car was a burnt-orange Honda Element with easily over 190,000 miles on the odometer. It was covered in so many bumper stickers that you would look at it and automatically think, "I bet that person believes in more conspiracy theories than I do." With her hippie machine fully packed with hiking sticks, books, camping gear, and an ever present Zen rock collection on her dashboard (that's not a joke), it wasn't long before the city skyline of her home began to shrink in the rearview mirror.

Driving around the speed limit in the slow lane, Laurie had been on the road about forty-five minutes when she noticed a white car to her immediate left. This car was drifting as though it was about to make a lane change, moving as if Laurie wasn't there at all. Laurie laid on the horn, but the white car continued to move into Laurie's lane without hesitation.

To avoid a collision at seventy miles per hour, Laurie swerved hard to the right. To avoid careening into the ditch, she immediately tried to correct her trajectory by pulling the wheel to the left. At that speed, her car lost control. The last thing Laurie remembered was feeling the roll begin. Her SUV flipped violently side over side down the highway, rolling four or five times before landing right-side up and backward on the freeway.

The person who caused this accident never stopped driving. A Good Samaritan who had seen the whole thing followed that white car to a gas station to ensure their information was documented. They asked the woman driving the white car if she realized what she had done. She responded affirmatively, said she had to pee, and went into the bathroom.

Meanwhile, Laurie was unconscious and trapped in her battered SUV. After she was pulled out of the vehicle, Laurie was flown by helicopter to MetroHealth Medical Center where a medical team rushed her to the emergency room. She had broken a rib, her head was lacerated, and she was suffering from internal bleeding. Laurie would require three days of treatment in the intensive care unit followed by two days in a regular trauma room.

Amanda, our cofounder, and I visited Laurie in the hospital as soon as we found out. By this time, Laurie was alert but still in pain. She told us about the terrible nature of the crash.

But then she mentioned something that both Amanda and I had forgotten. Laurie reminded us of a Promise Card she had written in one of our weekly staff meetings a while back. She had received several recall notifications in the mail from the manufacturer, alerting her to the defective airbags in Honda Elements. Shards of metal shrapnel were flying into people's chests, causing a major safety concern. Honda had recalled more than 1.2 million vehicles so that the airbags could be replaced. This letter was just noise in the volume of mail Laurie received, simply another annoying errand that she kept putting off. Finally, one day she needed a good promise for our staff meeting. She committed to replacing the faulty driver's side airbag in her car, and if it weren't for that promise, she might not be alive today. It's a good thing that she is a woman of her word.

Laurie made a strong recovery, and she came back to work almost two months later. She continued to work with us, until one day she came into my office and delivered the news that she needed to put in her two-week notice. Laurie accepted a new position fundraising for MetroHealth, the hospital that saved her life. We were sad to see her leave, but we understood why she needed to go.

The driver of the white car was charged with two felony counts regarding leaving the scene of a near-fatal accident. She eventually apologized for her actions, and Laurie accepted that apology. Laurie said, "It was genuine. It was terrifying. And it is healing."

The manufacturer recall that needs attention, that annoying beep of a smoke detector, the sharp corner in the garage that needs to be covered—the small steps we take to keep our families and ourselves safe should not be taken lightly. Little things feel little until one day they are big. By that time, it may be too late. ■

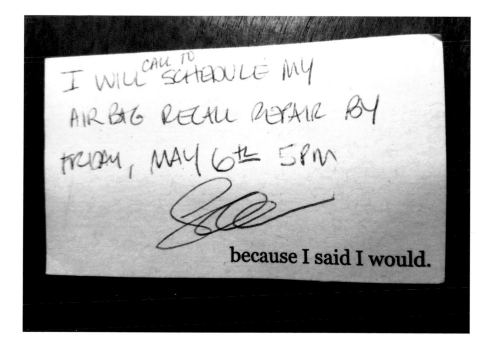

John's Ugly Tie

Football in Texas Can Make You Do Some Funny Things

John Bookman grew up playing football in Fort Worth, Texas. Back in the 1970s, when he was a kid, there was an organization in Fort Worth called the Panther Boys Club that helped local children grow up to be strong citizens. The club itself was located in a downtrodden area, right next to a homeless shelter. It had a couple of boxing rings and punching bags, and that was about it. But the club did its best and ran a lot of different programs, including youth football, which John played in.

One day, when John was in middle school, the Panther Boys Club football team had a game against a highly prestigious private school, the Fort Worth Country Day. The kids from Fort Worth Country Day were driven in a shiny, well-maintained bus that had probably never been driven down such unkept streets before. The Country Day players had new uniforms and good haircuts, and beside them the Panther boys looked a little shabby. But the cleanliness of your uniform does not define how well you can play the game. The Panthers were just better— or as John good-humoredly recalled later, "We beat the socks off the tea sippers at Country Day."

It would have been hard for the coaches from Country Day not to notice how good some of the Panther players were, and that observation would mark a turning point in John's life. One of the Country Day coaches took a personal interest in these kids and figured that if they had the academic ability to match their athletic skills, they should be offered a place at Country Day. Through the coach's efforts, a handful of boys were offered scholarships and would ultimately come to attend Fort

Worth Country Day. John Brookman was one of the boys chosen.

Brad Corbett Sr.

As John settled in to his new school, he not only got to know his new teammates but he also made lifelong friendships. At the time, the school was small, with only a couple hundred students; the new students got to know people pretty quickly. John soon struck up a deep friendship with one of his classmates and fellow players, Brad Corbett Jr.

When we make a childhood friend, we usually get to know something of their parents, too. John got to know Brad Jr.'s father very well—over time, counting him as a valuable mentor in his life. John describes Brad Sr. as a force of nature. Not only was he a big guy physically but he was also an extroverted salesman and businessman extraordinaire.

A tough kid from the Bronx, Brad Sr. had gone on to become a successful Texas businessman who was able to share what he had learned from his experiences with John. John described the essence of Brad Sr.'s perspective to me: "You have to be agile enough to learn from mistakes and get better from them. A fear of failure can fuel you so that you outwork everybody, which is positive, but it can also limit you because of the risks you *don't* take." He taught John the value of *failing forward*: learning from what went wrong and using it to your advantage.

Parents, of course, say many things, but Brad Corbett Sr. was an adult you might want to listen to. He had achieved a lot and was very successful in life. How successful? In 1974, Brad Sr. bought the Texas Rangers Major League Baseball team. Yes, Brad Sr. was born in the Bronx and grew up in Queens, and he loved his New York teams. But life brought him to Texas, so that's where one of his sports dreams would come true.

Some thirty years after learning life lessons from his friend's dad, John Brookman volunteers his time as a youth football coach, working with kids between the ages of ten and thirteen years old. From his own experience, John knows how significant a coach's guidance can be.

If you've ever hung around boys of that age, you know that they don't want to look foolish in front of each other. "They don't want to run a drill at full speed because they're afraid they'll fall and look silly, and when they do, the other guys will laugh at them," John explains. "We are very attentive to that, because it's the biggest inhibitor of their growth in learning the sport. If they're not willing to give it an all-out effort, even if they might fall down, they will never learn. We don't tolerate anyone laughing at somebody because they didn't do their drill right." This is John's lesson about failure for those boys, but in many ways, it's a lesson that came directly from his mentor, Brad Corbett Sr.

John honors Brad Sr. through his coaching style, but secretly John knew there was a serious character flaw in his mentor that he would never want his boys to share: Brad Sr. was a New York Giants fan. For readers who may not be familiar with why this is a problem, the Dallas Cowboys and the New York Giants are both in the same division (the NFC East) and by definition are rivals. John has lived his entire life about twenty miles from where the Dallas Cowboys play. Even after Brad Sr. lived in Texas for many years, and even though he had laid his money on a baseball team in Texas, when it came to football, Brad Sr. couldn't forget growing up in the Bronx, cheering for the New York Giants. He had absolutely no fear in rooting for his favorite team even when he was deep into enemy territory. In 2011, Brad Sr. even went as far as to give John a New York Giants tie for Christmas. Of course, John accepted the gift with a laugh, but he said later, "It just sat in the closet. I might have thought about blowing my nose on it, but I wasn't going to *wear* it."

Just one year later, at age seventy-five, Brad Corbett Sr. quietly passed away in his sleep, on Christmas Eve 2012. John Brookman wore that New York Giants tie for the very first time at his mentor's funeral.

Ever since that day, two times a year, John gets disapproving looks from strangers as he walks through his hometown of Fort Worth, Texas. Still a staunch Dallas Cowboys fan, John proudly wears that New York Giants tie

every time the two teams play. He wears it in memory of a man who helped shape him into the person he is today. Sure, he still thinks the tie is ugly, but it symbolizes a loyalty that runs deeper even than football in Texas.

Appreciation for a mentor can be expressed by wearing a ribbon, a pin, or even an ugly tie. But perhaps one of the most beautiful ways to honor our mentors in life is to pass their legacy on in the form of the lessons they have taught you. Who in your life has guided you along the way? What did they teach you? If you haven't already, maybe it's time to take that torch and find a way to pass it forward. ■

The Courage of No

Jenn's Promise to Her Friend Lucky

O ne evening in the fall of 2016, I was packing up my computer after a *because I said I would* chapter meetup while our chapter members were standing around chatting. As I was zipping up my backpack, one of our members, Jenn Dziak, approached me. "I'd like to tell you a story," she said to me. "But if I could tell you in private, would that be okay?" Jenn then told me the story that I have been given permission to tell you now.

Jenn had a very close friend named Lucky. Jenn and Lucky were drawn together in part by something they had in common. Both Jenn and Lucky struggled with depression. It is hard to fully understand this mental health challenge if you haven't been there yourself, but Jenn did her best to describe it to me. "It feels like you're in the wrong world," she said simply.

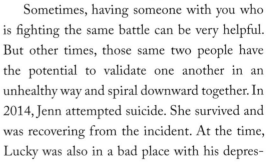

because I said I would.

Sometimes, having someone with you who is fighting the same battle can be very helpful. But other times, those same two people have the potential to validate one another in an unhealthy way and spiral downward together. In 2014, Jenn attempted suicide. She survived and was recovering from the incident. At the time, Lucky was also in a bad place with his depression and text messaged her trying to be supportive. He offered to kill himself with Jenn the next time she attempted suicide, so she didn't have to go alone. Jenn immediately knew this was not a healthy conversation. Even though she had just attempted suicide, her mind was in a better place at the moment, and she recognized how disturbing Lucky's offer was. As Jenn reflected on that text conversation, she told me, "I should have said no. I should have stopped him right there. If he really felt that way, then he needed to seek help." Unfortunately, we don't always have enough strength to do what we should in moments like these. On that day in 2014, Jenn looked at her phone and replied, "If you ever need someone to go with you, I will. I promise."

After this conversation, a year passed without incident. During this time, Jenn learned about *because I said I would*. She started volunteering at our headquarters, counting Promise Cards and mailing them to people who requested them.

On the day before Thanksgiving 2015, Lucky called Jenn in a state of severe depression. When they spoke, Jenn could hear the suicidal tendencies in his tone and words. Jenn was already worried about Lucky because she had seen Lucky posting to a Facebook group about his mental health, reaching out for help. On that phone call, Jenn told Lucky that life is worth living and that she was going to be there for him. She was a supportive friend and talked with him for three hours that day. She hung up the phone with a semblance of relief, thinking that her friend was in a better place.

To this day, Jenn still thinks about that conversation with Lucky, because unfortunately, it was their last. Later that night, Lucky used his brother's gun to shoot himself. He is survived by his daughter, who at that time was four months old.

Lucky's funeral was held on December 19, 2015. It was raining that day. "It felt like the world was crying with us," Jenn said. The loss was devastating to Lucky's other friends and his family, but Jenn's despair came from an additional place. It seemed to her that with every day she lived, she was breaking her promise to Lucky to commit suicide if he did. For a long time, she felt like she was disgracing her friend's memory, but Jenn soon changed her mind after becoming a *because I said I would* chapter member. *Because I said I would* is guided by a Code of Honor that defines compassion as our most important principle:

> "My belief in the importance of a promise is strong; however, I know that doing what is right will always be more important than keeping a promise. Commitment holds me accountable to my compassion; it does not blind me of it."

Jenn came to realize that she should have never made that promise to Lucky in the first place.

Coincidently, the very evening Jenn decided to tell me her story for the first time, the chapter did a personal development workshop on a subject we call the Courage of No. We had talked about the importance of saying no to commitments that we cannot or should not honor and the effects of social pressure. That night, we discussed the Milgram Study, an experiment conducted at Yale University in 1961 that showed how easily individuals can be pressured into doing something that they know is not right. This famous study set out to answer one question: "For how long will someone continue to give electric shocks to another person if they are told to do so, even if they think that other person could be seriously hurt?"[17] Our natural human tendencies to give in to pressure can be startling. Many people in that study would "shock" someone to apparent death just because an authority figure told them to.

Life pressures us in many ways, and sometimes that pressure can even come from friends. Our chapter talked about tactical ways we could practice the Courage of No in everyday life, even if it was in mundane situations, such as dealing with a telemarketer.

Jenn wishes she'd had the Courage of No on the day Lucky asked her to commit suicide with him. "I can't bring him back, but maybe

---

17   Susan Whitbourne, "The Secret Behind Psychology's Most Famous Experiment: What you didn't know about the Milgram experiments but thought you did," *Psychology Today*, January 22, 2013, https://www.psychologytoday.com/us/blog/fulfillment-any-age/201301/the-secrets-behind-psychology-s-most-famous-experiment.

I can stop someone else," she says. During a chapter meetup, Jenn made a personal promise to become a trained volunteer for the Crisis Text Line.[18] Many people who are depressed, especially younger people, are more comfortable talking about their feelings and experiences through text messages. The Crisis Text Line supports people in their most desperate times, helping them through mental health challenges, depression, and suicidal thoughts.

As you might guess, despair strikes hardest in the dark hours of the night and into the early morning. The time between 4:00 and 6:00 a.m. is when the greatest number of people reach out for support. But volunteering at 4:00 a.m. is not something most people want to do. That slot has a tremendously high demand, yet volunteers are in low supply. That is where Jenn found her place.

Like any good promise, her commitment required more than just well-intentioned emotions. It required contemplation and planning. On evenings before Jenn's early morning volunteer shifts, she would set her coffee timer, lay out all of her clothes, prepare her breakfast, and pack her lunch in advance. She would check the weather to ensure the clothes she laid out were the right ones. She even placed her computer next to her bed, so that when she woke up, it was right there. Not only are all those steps an incredible example of contemplation, but Jenn actually calendared out each and every one of them in separate entries to ensure that she would have enough time to be prepared. This included going to sleep before 8:30 p.m., so she would have enough energy to fulfill her 4:00 a.m. promise and go to work after.

"I feel so bad. I want to hold them," she tells me of the people she helps. In a way, she does.

Over the course of her time volunteering for the Crisis Text Line, Jenn Dziak has had text conversations with more than 120 people in desperate need. Depression affects people from all walks of life. Jenn

---

18   To contact the Crisis Text Line in the United States, text 741741.

does her best to help them, and she knows she makes an impact. In fact, after one exchange where the texter indicated to Jenn that they were actively in the process of ending their life, emergency services were dispatched to the texter's house. Jenn kept trying to engage with the texter until help arrived. That individual stayed alive that night, and I believe that Jenn Dziak's existence is part of the reason for that.

By being a part of this movement at a local level, Jenn realizes that it's not *just* about making any promises. It's about making the right ones. She says that she will spend the rest of her life breaking that promise she made to Lucky every single day—not in spite of him, but in honor of him.

Rest in peace, Lucky. ■

Honesty

· ·

Mahatma Gandhi once said, "Happiness is when what you think, what you say, and what you do are in harmony." Gandhi's wisdom has served the world in many ways, but this quote is challenging to agree with. Sometimes doing what you think is right doesn't result in happiness. Instead, it may speak truer to the definition of honesty than they do to the definition of happiness. Perhaps the most honest life is when our beliefs our words, and our actions are all in harmony.

Ask yourself this question: Are you who you say you are? A chapter member once mentioned this question to me in a conversation and the words have not left my memory since. Those seven words can spark profound introspection. Honesty is hard to get good at but its value in life has no parity. To understand that more deeply simply ask a wife or husband who has been cheated on.

It is unfortunate but true that dishonesty pays off for many in the short term. There are people who gain from lying and stealing. But a Russian proverb speaks to how this way of life ends in the long run. "With lies you may get ahead in the world, but you can never go back." Trust is the foundation of well-functioning families, relationships, economies, governments, and just about everything else. Many are far too willing to trade their trust for a fleeting moment.

It is interesting how some forms of dishonesty are commonly paired with genuinely good intentions. The people pleaser in us wants to make the other person happy by saying yes to commitments even if we don't mean it. For example, it might be common for you to extend an invitation to a friend and in response they quickly say, "Of course, I'll be there!" But how often are you confident that the person actually means what they are saying? Many people just say yes to get through a sticky point in a conversation, knowing full well that their promises will be broken later. Wanting people to be happy is a good thing, but remember that nobody is handing out favors by making promises they don't intend to keep. The person who makes the most promises often also breaks the most. Saying no to the wrong promise gives us the capacity to say yes to the right ones.

There is also the risk of being *too* honest. Almost no character value is absolute, and that includes honesty. A lot of parents have witnessed this firsthand with their own children. A young child may point at a person with a disorder or disability and start saying things r asking questions that they mean innocently but that can easily be aken as offensive. There are also many moments where the value of onesty is ambiguous. In a very different scenario, what are we to say o our significant other if the haircut really *doesn't* look good?

In moments of moral dilemma, there is a thought-provoking tac-ic that may prove useful. Try to combine two different elements of onor (yours or ours), and you may find an interesting perspective. or example, with the two preceding scenarios, you could combine onesty and compassion. Ask yourself, "Which value is more import-nt in this moment?" Or, better yet, "Can the two values be used in a neaningful balance?" Perhaps the parent apologizes to the stranger nd, later on, uses the situation as a teachable moment for their child. ust because something is true doesn't mean it needs to be said. Hon-sty should have a purpose. In regard to the bad haircut, maybe the pouse can respond (while still being honest) by saying that the last aircut was better, but he or she still looks beautiful. Sometimes, just nough honesty is all the world really needs. In other instances, a half-ruth is a whole lie. There is no magic formula. We just have to make a houghtful decision and live with the consequences, knowing we tried o do the right thing in a world where decisions aren't perfect. ∎

I seek to live a life where what I believe, what I say, and what I do are all in harmony. I should treat others the same way I think I should be treated. As I work to be honest with others, I cannot forget that I must also be honest with myself. The truth is often both hard to deliver and desperately needed.

because
I said
I would.

I will never ask anyone
to lie for me.

because I said I would.

I will
learn to swim...

because I said I would.

▼ **THIS PROMISE CARD** was written by a six-year-old girl in a home for children who have been neglected, abandoned, or abused.

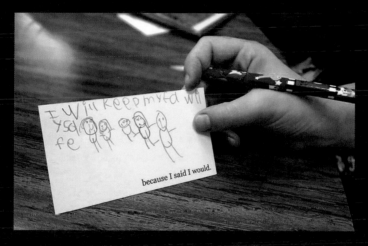

"I will keep my family safe."

▲ **A WALL OF PROMISE CARDS** made by high school students

▲ **PRECIOUS SINGO IS OUR CHAPTER LEADER** in Columbus, Ohio. She came to our first chapter meetup in Columbus and has stuck with us ever since. Not all chapters' efforts are successful. Like anything, a chapter takes hard work to make sustainable. Precious is the reason why the group is getting so large that we are having trouble finding a big enough room. Also, it's hard not to like someone named Precious. Like, how do you get angry at that?

▲ *BECAUSE I SAID I WOULD* **HAD THE HONOR** of presenting to the United States Air Force Academy in Colorado Springs, Colorado. This is a picture of the cadets eating lunch. The sandwiches were actually pretty good.

▲ **IN 2014,** I promised to volunteer at a different nonprofit for fifty-two weeks in a row. It was only two to four hours a week on average, but I learned more about how society functions through this experience than any other in my life.

▼ **THIS IS A PICTURE OF ME** from the week
I volunteered at the animal shelter. If those dogs
look guilty, it's because they pooped everywhere.

Thirty-Four Hundred Miles, Give or Take

Jay Promises to Walk across the United States

E very year across the nation, charities of all kinds host events—such as walks, marathons, and bike rides—to raise funds and awareness for their causes. They are admirable ventures, but sometimes the events—a walk, for example—can seem a little disconnected from the cause itself. The walk isn't going to literally stop cancer or end homelessness. It is supposed to be symbolic. But in the case of Jay's walk, he would literally come face-to-face with the particular cause he was fighting for. At the time of this story, Jay was in his early twenties. He has lived in Norristown, Pennsylvania, all of his life, except for 115 days in 2013, when he walked across the United States.

Jay

The idea came to Jay when he hit rock bottom in his life. By his own account, a cluster of bad decisions led him to drop out of college and drift into a life of hard drinking, drug use, run-ins with the law, and homelessness. Then one day at a bar, he met a girl who invited him to a church conference. Jay hadn't attended any kind of church since high school, but the trip sounded interesting, so he traveled to Atlanta with a group from the girl's church.

Sitting in the Georgia Dome stadium along with 60,000 other young people, Jay listened as a young girl took the stage and began talking about her experience being a victim of human trafficking, a modern version of slavery. As you read this story, there are nearly 21 million victims of forced labor in the world, according to the International Labor Organization. A quarter of them are under eighteen years of age.[19]

Maybe you already know about these realities, but this was the first time Jay had been confronted by this issue. The emotion of it overwhelmed him, and sitting there in that crowded stadium, his outlook on life changed. Jay had been at a crossroads, floating in a state free of responsibility. This speaker unknowingly provided the direction he was looking for. Together with his childhood friend Shannon, who was also drifting through life and looking for an adventure, Jay decided he was going to walk across the country to raise awareness for human trafficking.

Shannon (left) and Jay (right)

---

19 "The Facts," Polaris, Accessed on May 3, 2018, https://polarisproject.org/human-trafficking/facts.

Jay and Shannon started doing research on what route they should take. They spent hours in the library and consulted with ultra-athletes to understand what it would take to complete a walk like this. Routes were planned and weather patterns were accounted for.

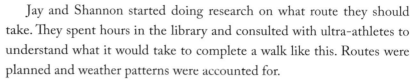

Just kidding. They didn't do anything like that. They just printed out a map from Google like they were going to Grandma's house and packed a bag of survival stuff like they were running away from home. Remember, kids, plan before you promise. On July 14, 2013, Jay and Shannon decided they would sleep on the beach in Atlantic City, New Jersey, before starting their walk. They found an abandoned lifeguard tower, which seemed like a perfect place to lay down their sleeping bags. Around midnight, though, a police officer shined his flashlight in their faces and told them to move on. Jay and Shannon found another spot and spent the night in the sand, digging down and covering themselves as best they could. With the chill and brine of the breeze coming off the shore, the reality of their journey set in immediately.

There are many moments from that long walk that characterize the wild nature of Jay and Shannon's promise to walk across the country. Some cities were very inviting; others weren't so welcoming. In one town in Pennsylvania, a man yelled at them using the N-word. They tried to shake it off, but that is easier said than done. Other times, the battles were much more on the comical side, like Shannon's up-close-and-personal encounter with a wild turkey.

Among such perilous meetings and entertaining moments, one episode has special significance for Jay. That is the focus of this story, and it happened in Topeka, Kansas.

Jay and Shannon had just hiked into town. As was so often the case, they were very, very hungry. These were long days on the road with limited resources. They saw a sign for a ten-dollar, all-you-can-eat buffet at the local Pizza Hut. It was too expensive for their budget, but sometimes we lack self-control. The two of them walked into the air-conditioned restaurant and began loading their plates. Then they sat down at a booth and ate until they could eat no more. Their stomachs full, they lingered over sodas, enjoying a respite from the beating sun.

Jay was seated facing the door when he saw two young women walk in, accompanied by a little girl and a man who seemed suspicious. It was as if he was watching out for something. The group took a table just behind Jay and Shannon. Then one of the young women came over and started chatting with them. The girl told them her name was Jessica, that she was with her cousin Melissa, and that the little girl with them was Melissa's daughter, Sara. Something about these girls—their skimpy clothes, their tattoos, the way Melissa seemed to need permission to speak with them—rang an alarm in Jay's mind.

As they were chatting, Melissa walked over and said something off-beat: She said that she was "in the life." Jay knew that this was code for prostitution. Jessica told them that Melissa was an escort on a website notorious as a hub for sex trafficking.

As Jay was trying to wrap his head around what was happening, Jessica made them an offer that was very hard to refuse: "Do you want to come back to Melissa's apartment and have a shower?" she asked. A shower was something Jay and Shannon hadn't had for many days. The prospect of cool, clean water and plenty of soap was incredibly tempting, but at the same time, Jay was thinking, *This situation sounds terrible. Two friends on a mission to take a stand against human trafficking stop to take a shower at a prostitute's apartment?*

To an outsider, it may have sounded like Jay and Shannon wanted something else, but they literally just wanted to take a shower and feel human again. They took a taxi and met the girls at Melissa's apartment.

It occurred to Jay after they got to Melissa's that he should be worried about Melissa's pimp, the man accompanying them at Pizza Hut, showing up. What would this man do if he thought these strangers were asking too many questions? Maybe this was more dangerous than Jay initially thought.

Sitting inside the apartment, Jay and Shannon talked with Melissa and Jessica. As they sat there, Jay remembered that young girl on the stage in Atlanta. Perhaps this was the moment that all those other moments were supposed to lead to. He explained why they were walking. "We can get you out of this life," Jay told Melissa. "We know some people in Topeka who can help you."

As they continued their discussion, a rusty orange truck cruised slowly past the building several times, the bass of the stereo so loud you could feel it. It was Melissa's pimp, Todd, checking in. Someone like Todd does not look kindly on nonpaying visitors. Jessica went outside to speak to him, and Jay and Shannon decided to play it safe by hiding under Sara's bed. Jay is a *big* guy—he barely made it under the child's bed frame. Sara was in bed still asleep, and every time Jay moved, the mattress swayed a bit like a mechanical bull.

A little while later, Jessica came back inside. Todd left, for the time being. But they couldn't relax. They only had a few hours at most before he would return. Melissa wanted to leave her situation, but she was afraid. Where would she go? Would she be safe from Todd? How would she support her daughter?

Jay calmed her fears by talking up his connections and what they could do for her. In his determination to help Melissa escape this life, Jay was exaggerating about how they could help, but he justified that internally: *Their life has to be better than this*. Eventually, Melissa agreed to leave, but there was a catch. She had to make sure the door to the apartment was locked behind them, because that was how Todd controlled her and made sure that she was still in the apartment. Melissa had no key to the door, so she couldn't lock it from the outside. It could only be locked from the inside.

"I can fix that," Jay told her. "Just go downstairs and call a taxi. I'll lock the door behind you." Jay sounded confident, so they believed him. Shannon, Melissa, Jessica, and Sara left the apartment, grabbing a few possessions on their way out. Jay locked the door behind them from the inside and then walked through the apartment to the balcony in the back.

Jay didn't actually have a plan. There was no magic way of locking that door behind them. The only way for the door to remain locked to fool Todd was for Jay to jump off the balcony. However, this apartment was on the third floor.

Despite all the walking, Jay was still around 240 pounds. As he looked out the window, he visualized himself swinging down like an American Ninja Warrior to the second-floor balcony and then to the first. Then he would be on the ground soon, with the crowd going wild.

Jay began to ease himself over the side of the balcony. Hanging by his hands, he grabbed hold of a light fixture beside the balcony, but it began to bend. It was going to snap if he put his weight on it, so Jay decided that was a bad idea. His plan was now to get his feet on the second-floor balcony railing, and just drop the rest of the way—at least he would fall only two floors instead of three.

As Melissa and Sara were rounding the corner of the apartment building, they were gifted with the vision of Jay's aerial majesty as he fell to the ground. He sat up and rubbed his chest, which hurt from his knees slamming into it. The cab driver they called had just pulled up and saw the whole thing too and he just shook his head. "That was crazy," he said. "I don't know what's going on here, but just get in and I'll take you where you need to go."

Jay was ultimately able to connect Melissa to an abolitionist organization that could provide her with the resources she needed to make a fresh start. As I write this, Melissa is living a regular life, completing her collegiate studies in nursing, with a steady boyfriend and a baby on the way. Four years after Jay helped Melissa, Jessica, and Sara escape "the life," Todd and his associates were indicted on human sex trafficking charges. If convicted, he could face life in prison.

After saying their farewells to the girls on that fateful day in Topeka, Jay and Shannon continued on their way, walking another 1,500 miles. They completed their epic journey on the beach in Santa Monica, California.

I want the story of this walk to sound like a promise fulfilled—an epic journey all the way across the country. But the truth is that Jay and Shannon got some rides along the way. Out of more than 3,400 miles in their total journey, Jay walked about 3,000 miles. Shannon threw in the towel just past Chicago but joined back up a week later. You might be feeling a tad disappointed, knowing that their promise was not fully kept. And that would be understandable. But they only deserve so much criticism. No, Jay and Shannon can't say they kept their promise, but they can say they changed someone's life forever. Sometimes even in failure there is victory. ■

Car Number Two

The Vacation of a Lifetime

Mary Connolly is a mother of three who is originally from Massachusetts. Mary describes one of her children, John, born in the mid-1980s, as an intelligent and self-driven child. Those qualities are best understood with an example. When John was in Little League Baseball, he quickly figured out that little kids throw the ball slowly and without accuracy. Even a single base hit can turn into an inside-the-park home run; all you have to do is keep running. The coach would yell for John to stop at a particular base, but little John knew the other little kids' throws were too sloppy to make it on time. He would ignore his coach's advice and keep running.

Mary on vacation

John grew up, graduated from college, and went to work for one of the world's largest consulting firms at their Boston office and then later at their New York City office. Many years after those Little League home runs, John is still the kind of person who sometimes defies the norm—even when it comes to something like taking a vacation. He doesn't like to go on stereotypical trips. He was better off skipping popular places like Italy or the Bahamas. John reasoned that one day he would probably get married, and his future wife would probably want to go to places like that. He thought that now was the time to go to countries like Ecuador, Iceland, and other locations, places his unknown soul mate might not be interested in.

For example, on the day John turned thirty-one, he was setting off on a much-anticipated trip to Portugal and Spain with his mom, Mary. He was excited to be visiting new places, and Mary was looking forward to this trip for reasons of her own. Four years earlier, she had ended her twenty-nine-year marriage to John's dad—she was experiencing a rough period in her life. "When a relationship that has lasted that long comes to an

Mary's son, John

end," Mary says, "it can feel like you are going through a grieving process for years afterward." She was used to being a mother and a wife, and now that focus had ended. Mary was living on her own for the very first time. She had entered the full-time workforce once more, knowing that she had to figure out a way to retire one day. Mary and John planned this trip to Portugal and Spain as a time to get away and reset the clock.

"It is ironic that my story ends at a hotel named My Story in the beautiful Rossio Square in Lisbon, Portugal. The hotel room became my sanctuary, where I could begin to process what had happened to my son, John, and I earlier in the day. A day I can never forget, a day I'm still struggling to understand. Friday, September 9, the day we survived a train derailment and crash in O Porriño, Spain."

Mary describes the start of this trip far differently than its ending. The vacation began as picturesque. They rented an apartment in Bairro Alto, a quaint little neighborhood in Lisbon, the capital of Portugal. Shaking off their jet lag, they rode a tourist bus around the city to see the main sites. In the coastal city of Porto, they took a cruise down the Douro River and stopped at a neighborhood wine bar to eat local charcuterie.

On the morning of Friday, September 9, 2016, after a week of visiting various cities and sites in Portugal and Spain, Mary and John were traveling back to Lisbon for their flights home. They were walking to the train station in Vigo, a scenic port city in the south of Spain. Mary packed far too much for the trip and her suitcase was chubby. "The wheels finally broke from the constant dragging over cobblestones," Mary recalls. "John switched bags with me and dragged my heavy, over-packed bag while I dragged his light, easy bag down the hill to the train station." They arrived at the station, found their train, and got into car number two.

When they found their seats, John had to lift Mary's overstuffed bag up onto the luggage rack above their heads. "The two gentlemen who were sitting in the row across from us suggested that we move my suitcase because it was hanging over the edge of the rack," Mary says, reflecting on the moment. "One of the men said his wife was uncomfortable because the bag was over her and if the train jerked too much, it may fall on her. John was stressed and his arms were hurting from lifting the bag, so I tried to joke with them, stating the bag wasn't going anywhere because it weighed too much."

This little shot of humor got Mary the laugh she was looking for. The situation was neutralized, and they sat down. Right on time, the train left the station. Both John and Mary were tired from many late nights on their incredible trip, so they tried to nap as the train moved along.

All of a sudden, the train jerked to the left.

It was enough to wake most of the dozing passengers. They looked around, and perhaps some of them reasoned that the train was old, so this was to be expected. There are bumps and jolts on any train ride, right? But then, the train jerked hard to the right and confusion set in with the passengers. At this point, they knew something was wrong. Mary and John looked at each other, alarm starting to show in their faces.

Next, the train violently jerked back to the left and everything started shaking. The noise was terrifying. "This is the moment where my concept of time changed from normal to very slow motion," Mary says.

"During the events that followed, I had to remind myself to breathe to calm myself down, because I kept forgetting to breathe. This was something that ten years of yoga has taught me—that your breath will help you in any situation, just breathe.

"People were getting thrown from their seats. All of the suitcases were falling from the luggage rack onto the people below. John and I look at each other because reality has hit and we knew that we were on a train that was crashing. I started to feel myself coming out of my seat, and my mind was screaming, *No, no, no, you do not want to come out of your seat. This is not good. Try to resist falling. Stop!* I had no control over what was happening to my body—in very slow motion, I was coming out of my seat and falling. I do not remember hitting the floor, nor the violent motion of being spun around to face the back of the train. I am sure this torquing and twisting motion was what caused the injuries I sustained.

"After leaving my seat, the next thing I remember is being in the aisle, on my butt, facing backward. I saw my son still in his seat. He was screaming, 'Mom!' and I was screaming, 'John!' as I was being pulled down the aisle away from him by a force I cannot resist, away from him, not being able to control the motion or direction I am being pulled. We were staring and screaming at each other, and I am sure the look of terror and disbelief I see on John's face is the same look reflected on my face to John. I remember in that moment thinking, *Oh my God, please do not let John watch me die. Oh my God, please do not let me watch my son John die. Oh my God, we are both going to die.*

"Just as quickly as the crash began, the train stopped. John jumped up from his seat to help me get up. We knew we had just survived a train crash, so we hugged each other like never before. We made sure that we were both okay. We were.

"Then the screaming of the other passengers brought us back to reality. People were hurt—some really bad. The old gentleman who was sitting across from me asked us to help his wife, who was also thrown from her seat. John and I picked her up from the floor and got her back in her seat; she assured us she was fine. Her husband, however, was not okay. He kept saying in a strangely calm voice, 'I think I broke my leg. It is really bad.'"

Many of the passengers were injured. The woman in the last row of the train car was bleeding from her head, and her left arm was hanging down by her side, twisted in an unnatural way. John stood up out of his seat and went to the train door to see if he could help anyone. Mary didn't want to be left alone, but she kept those feelings to herself. Those feelings were only amplified by what she saw next.

"When I turned around, I saw it. I was looking out the window, toward the embankment. I wasn't sure what I saw at first. It did not look human. It looked like a stuffed old scarecrow that had been thrown out to the curb after Halloween. One part of my brain is saying, *What is that?* and the other part of my brain is saying, *You know what it is.* This inner dialogue continues for a while. It is grey, swollen, and dusty. The head is at a weird angle, and the limbs are not all attached, which is why my brain does not want to recognize what I am seeing."

Sixty-two passengers were on that train. Four died, and forty-nine were injured.

The following day, Mary and John flew home. There are no trains where Mary lives in Ohio; she drives mostly. John, however, lives in New York City and takes the train to work every day. On the phone with me, Mary reflects that she still can't believe her son was able to move on so eas-

ily. Mary's way of moving on was a little different. The train crash reminded her that life can be taken from us at any moment, and she wanted to do something to leave her mark on the world. She began looking for volunteer opportunities. Mary found out about our local chapter of *because I said I would* in her city and decided to join.

"I joined *because I said I would* in December 2016 and have enjoyed the monthly meetups and volunteer opportunities that I have been able to attend. It is true that you get more than you give. I always feel happy on the days I am able to volunteer and help someone else. My life is improving daily, and I cannot wait to enjoy each day and see how the rest of my story will be written. One of my promises was to finish *this* story. I am happy to complete this promise and to start the next."

And that's what she did. At a chapter meetup, Mary made the promise to write the story of what happened to her on that train. Across the spectrum of human experience, there are many ways to go about recovery, whether it's art therapy, seeing a psychologist, or simply writing your story down. Mary had been struggling to get her words down on paper, because every time she would start, the emotions she experienced during the crash would flood back, and she would begin to cry. The promise to write down her story, parts of which are included in these pages, was her way of addressing her emotions. We all have to find our own way forward. ■

I will write.
I will put pen to paper and purge
my soul of all that I have been
through, no matter how painful
it may be.

because I said I would.

Soda Toast

Jeremy's Family Goes to Disney World

There is something really magical about Walt Disney World. Sure, the whole Disney thing can be over-the-top and even unreasonably materialistic, but it is an experience that we quickly justify for the happiness of a child. Maybe it's because as adults it's hard to have that sense of wonder again, so if we can't have it we want to give it to someone who can. Jeremy Allinger wanted his two sons, Quinton and Caden, to feel that magic. "In my heart of hearts, I feel like every child deserves to experience Disney," Jeremy once told me.

Quinton (left) and Caden (right)

However, Jeremy had an oddly specific reason to make the trip in 2012 with his wife, Stephanie, and their boys. It was something that seems silly now, but it felt real back then. With half a smile and a dash of embarrassment, Jeremy said, "It was around 2012, and I was certain the apocalypse was going to happen. I was determined to get them there before it happened." When Jeremy told me this, we laughed. He was referring to the ancient Mayan calendar that shows a major era ending around December 21, 2012. Some people back then genuinely believed that this meant the end of the world.

He laughs about it now, but back then he was determined to get his boys to Disney World before the apocalypse. So, they traveled from their home in Jordan, Minnesota, to Florida for the most magical vacation of their boys' lives. Quinton, then four years old, and Caden, who had just turned three, were finally old enough to truly enjoy the rides, the costumed characters, and the shows. The family even stayed in one of those overpriced Disney properties. After all, the apocalypse was coming and money would be toilet paper soon anyway.

There was just one thing that wasn't quite perfect in paradise, though. Even long before this trip, Quinton had been getting cold- and flu-like symptoms that lasted for maybe a week then disappeared. And then a week later, they would come back. So on this trip to Florida, it was not a surprise to Jeremy and Stephanie that Quinton got a nighttime cough. Nevertheless, they decided that when they got back home, they should pay a visit to the doctor. When they returned to Minnesota, Jeremy made an appointment and took Quinton to their pediatrician with Caden in tow.

The doctor started her examination of young Quinton. "He's certainly looking very pale," she said. She took hold of his fingertips and squeezed.

She was looking to see whether Quinton's skin would return to its normal color quickly. If his fingers stayed red, that could be a sign of a blood-deficiency issue. What she saw prompted her to take a sample of Quinton's blood and send it to the lab.

The doctor completed her evaluation and left the room for what felt like a long time but was perhaps only half an hour. That's still a long time for young children, so Quinton and Caden got busy playing with the toys that the pediatrician's office supplied for moments just like this.

The doctor came back into the room and closed the door behind her. She looked at the two boys and said in a stern voice, "I need you guys to be quiet because I have to talk to your dad for a second." Jeremy's heart sank; he knew something serious was happening. This is not the way the doctor usually spoke to him.

"There is definitely something wrong with his blood," she told Jeremy. "It could be anything from a viral infection to leukemia."

In these situations, some parents understandably go into immediate denial, but Jeremy just started to cry. Before they came to the pediatrician's office, he had done what most parents would do; Jeremy researched Quinton's symptoms online. The word *leukemia* kept popping up—a type of blood cancer that makes the body produce increased numbers of abnormal blood cells. This means the bone marrow can't produce enough of the healthy white blood cells the body needs to fight infection. For many, it is a terminal disease.

As Jeremy tried to take in this news, he looked down. His two boys were still playing. Their father's world was being torn apart, but they were totally unaware of the life-threatening news that had just been delivered. It was as if there were two different worlds in that very same room.

Jeremy called Stephanie to join them, and together the family went straight to the children's hospital in Minneapolis. There, the reality of what was happening hit Jeremy hard. "When you get to the seventh floor of this hospital, there's a sign that says *Children's Oncology Unit*, and it begins to sink in." *Children* and *oncology*. Those words should never be so close together. Even now, the diagnosis was not certain, but that moment would come soon enough.

By sheer good fortune, Quinton's case was assigned to a highly respected and experienced pediatric oncologist. They were in excellent hands, but this doctor did not have good news for them.

"Well, I've looked at his blood and I can tell you with every certainty in my mind that it is leukemia," the oncologist told them.

That day, Quinton had surgery to install a Hickman line, a rubber tube inserted into the neck or chest to deliver the kinds of medications needed in chemotherapy.

"That long tube sticking out of his chest was kind of shocking to see," Jeremy recalled to me later, wincing at the memory. Medical tubing on a child's skin seemed inhuman. But with the Hickman line in place, Quinton's treatment would start immediately.

So the Allinger family's cancer journey began. They spent most of the next six months living out of a tiny hospital room. They were right by Quinton's side as he went through bout after bout of chemotherapy,

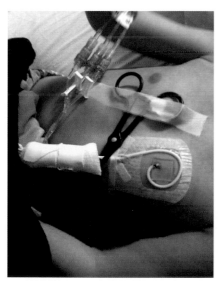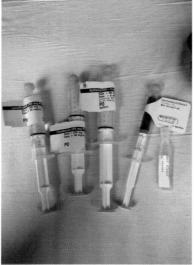

attempting to defeat the cancer in his blood-forming tissues. Their daily lives worked to a different timetable now, determined by Quinton's treatment. Through the long nights, Jeremy and Stephanie had many serious conversations and even unspoken moments of understanding about the situation. They shared the fear and the reality that perhaps they would have to bury their son.

As news reached their family and friends, visitors and care packages poured in. Support also came from unexpected channels at times. Jeremy's friend Adam became a regular visitor; every time he came, he took Jeremy and Stephanie out to lunch, and he brought video games for Quinton to play, easing the monotony of a long hospital stay.

"Adam was the one that really surprised me," Jeremy says. "You expect family to be there, but for someone like him, to go as far as he did . . . . He's like a brother to me now. I'm forever grateful for what he did for us."

When life is so uncertain, sometimes people—both friends and strangers—default to making promises, seeking to make things right (or at least better). People promised to send gifts or to visit the family in the hospital. In an effort to brighten the bleak days, Jeremy and Stephanie would tell Quinton about a visitor who said they would be coming that day or some treat they would be bringing him. It's curious how a promise works. A promise can both give hope and take it away, because many of those visitors and those gifts never came. Getting cancer is not a choice—even a child can understand that—but when someone breaks a promise to you, it feels like they made their choice. That's really hard for a kid in the hospital to accept.

Ultimately, though, this story ends the way you want it to. The treatments worked. At age five, Quinton completed his last course of chemotherapy. In that hospital room at 11:10 p.m., Jeremy watched the last dose of blue medication flow until the bag was empty. To celebrate this long-awaited moment, the family toasted with bottles of Pepsi.

Jeremy and his family have a duty to be thankful to those who showed up for them during their crisis. They also have every right to be disappointed in those who didn't. But we should dwell on disappointment for

only so long. At some point, we need to move on and let that disappointment become part of a change for the benefit of ourselves or for others.

Reflecting on this most unfortunate journey, Jeremy decided to make a promise to himself: "Tons of people promised to help us with stuff but never did. I'll never do that same thing to anybody." ■

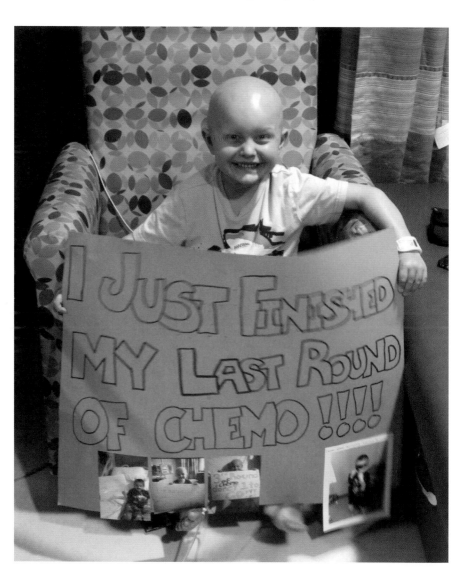

Accountability

WILLINGNESS TO ACCEPT PERSONAL RESPONSIBILITY

1. Self-Control
2. Compassion
3. Contemplation
4. Honesty
5. **Accountability**
6. Sacrifice
7. Hope

Taking personal responsibility for our actions is important because, even though it hurts sometimes, accountability is an incredible tool for personal growth. When we accept accountability for our successes or failures, we learn. If we do not learn how to take responsibility with grace, the personal development process breaks down. How can a person ever get better if they can never accept when they are wrong?

Unfortunately, holding someone accountable is not often executed with improvement in mind. When a promise is broken to someone, there is a tendency for that person to want some form of justice or retribution. A broken promise can be heartbreaking, and sometimes we want the other person to feel the same disappointment. But if we are shouting at someone because of their failure, and the *only* thing we want is a sense of personal validation, then maybe we are the ones who need to be held accountable for our self-control.

I am sure that Jeremy Allinger felt a strong sense of anger when people broke promises to his little boy who had leukemia. Jeremy could have easily embarrassed those people on social media for letting down a child stricken with cancer. But instead of doing that, he took his disappointment as a personal reminder that he needed to support other families with children in the hospital, which he has done. The difference between accountability and retribution lies in the pursuit of improvement.

Unfortunately, it's hard to hold people accountable these days because many react negatively when confronted, even when it's done in a reasonable and respectful manner. Many individuals simply cannot handle an honest account of their mistakes. Some simply shut down and walk away from the situation or some may end the relationship entirely. Others can lash out in anger, turning the criticism back on other parties as a defense mechanism. This describes someone who has a low accountability threshold.

Accountability threshold is a term that we use at *because I said I would* to describe the level of tolerance and acceptance that someone has for honest and accurate feedback on their performance in a promise. A person who has a high accountability threshold is someone you want know. This person quickly acknowledges their shortfalls without resistance. This rare character will even admit a weakness that they can barely admit to themselves.

Before starting a conversation with someone about what went wrong in a situation, ask yourself how high or low you think the person's accountability threshold is. In other words, what words would push this person over the edge or damage your relationship? The next question is the tougher one. Which do you value more in this situation: the principle of accountability for one's action or the relationship itself? You are ultimately left with the following choices:

- Do not hold the person accountable at all and avoid the conversation. Keep the relationship and attempt to forgive the person internally. Do not value accountability in this particular moment.

- Hold the personal accountable with gentle words that are not as strong as you really feel but that at least provide some accountability. Value accountability some, but the relationship more.

- Be direct with your words in a way that holds the person justifiably accountable and accept the risk of losing the relationship. Value accountability more than the relationship.

As a leader, it is hard to teach accountability. There is a quote from Albert Einstein that can point us in the right direction, though:

> "Setting an example is not the main means of influencing others, it is the only means."

Strong leaders show others that it's socially acceptable to accept accountability by admitting their own faults. These social cues build a culture of humility that can serve the greater good.

Research suggests that accountability also has a positive impact on goal-attainment rates. Psychology professor Dr. Gail Matthews of the Dominican University of California found that sharing goals with others proves to be incredibly beneficial. In a study of 267 participants, she found that if a person held themselves accountable to a goal by sending updates to a friend, they were two times more likely to achieve their objective compared to those who did not have an accountability partner.[20]

The reason peer-to-peer accountability works well may come down to biology.

Prehistoric humans found it very difficult to survive in the natural world alone. To overcome the physical weaknesses of a single person, humans consolidated their strength by forming tribes. *Fight one of us and you'll have to fight us all*, they reasoned. They warded off predators, they endured the weather, and they built villages together because they had to. You had to keep the respect of other people in the tribe because if you didn't, you could be banished from the tribe. Left to fight alone, your likelihood of survival diminished severely, and many who took this path died. It stands to reason, then, that those who did care about what the rest of the tribe thought lived on, had children, and handed those same attributes to a new generation. Over time, accountability became a part of human nature. Although this dynamic may no longer be such a strong part of human survival, functions of those instincts still appear to be with us. Use them to your advantage. Tell other people of your promises. Post them to social media if you have to. Commit to check-ins with friends, and let's put our instincts to work.

The thought of accountability cannot end without recognizing an unfortunate but simple fact: Everybody breaks promises, and that

---

20 "Study Focuses on Strategies for Achieving Goals, Resolutions," Dominican University of California, Accessed on May 3, 2018. https://www.dominican.edu/dominicannews/study-highlights-strategies-for-achieving-goals.

cludes me and you. Unforeseen factors appear out of nowhere, sometimes, our planning falls short. Our internal drive and motivation has its limits. The only way to not break any promises is to not make any, and quite frankly, that is the life of a coward. We all make mistakes; that's not the challenge. The challenge is whether you genuinely feel remorse about your shortfalls and whether you are going to do anything about them. ∎

CODE OF HONOR:

Accountability

I must be willing to accept personal responsibility for what I have done and what I have failed to do—both in what is good and what is not. Accountability helps me understand that my decisions have consequences. I help hold others accountable, but before I become too upset with the broken promises of others, I remember that I too have weaknesses.

because
I said
I would.

▲ Ann and her niece

New Years Promise: Plant flowers on my grandparents and uncles grave.

New Years Promise: I will tell 10 people they are beautiful.

New Years Promise: Drink only water for a week.

New Years Promise: I will talk to my cousin for the first time.

New Years Promise: I will make my mom breakfast 1 day.

New Years promise: I will Ask more questions in classes.

▲ **EMMA MADE FIFTY-TWO PROMISES** to kick off her New Year. Each week, she would randomly grab one of the promises out of the bowl where she kept her Promise Cards, and she gave herself one week to fulfill her commitment. She recorded a video each week about how things went. All fifty-two promises were kept. #MomVerified

I will write letters to every single one of my teachers K-12 to show my appreciation. because I said I would.

▲ **ABOUT 357,000 AMERICANS** have sudden cardiac arrest outside of a hospital each year. Only 12 percent of those people survive. CPR can nearly triple the survival rates for these victims by helping support life until emergency responders arrive. In our dedication to citizenship, multiple *because I said I would* chapters have held CPR certification training for their members. The woman in the red sleeveless shirt is Mary Connolly, the chapter member who survived the train crash in Spain.

▲ **ON AVERAGE, CHILDREN** in foster care move one to two times *each year.*[21] New school. New classes. Each move makes it harder to graduate. Members of the Columbus, Ohio, chapter of *because I said I would* wanted to make life a little easier for kids struggling through these challenges, so they made a promise to purchase and assemble new bikes for foster care kids. We threw a pizza party and surprised the kids with their new rides.

---

21 American Bar Association and Casey Family Programs, *Questions and Answers: Credit Transfer and School Completion,* Legal Center for Foster Care & Education, 2008, https://www.americanbar.org/content/dam/aba/migrated/child/education/QA_2_Credits_FINAL.authcheckdam.pdf.

I Promise to wash myhair

because I said I would.

I will feed my family
more REAL
FOOD!

because I said I would.

▲ Kimchi, the *because I said I would* office dog

◀ **PAUL HAS ONLY** one tattoo. With his sleeves rolled up, a lady at the bar glances at it and smiles. "Did you lose a bet?" she says.

"No," Paul says with a little laugh.

Paul told a friend that he would get a tattoo. The day of the visit to the tattoo parlor was nearing, and he had narrowed it down to two choices. "I didn't want a flag or a picture," Paul remembers thinking.

He wrote us a message about what he ultimately chose to go with." Just over two years ago, in the midst of personal turmoil, I found your Facebook page, and it changed my life. I used it as motivation to get myself in better shape. A few months later, I was diagnosed with cancer. I used it to motivate me to survive . . . and I did. Now, it's literally a permanent part of me. Thank you for helping me understand how important it is to follow through on promises."

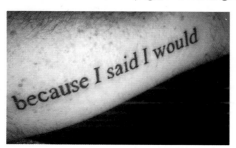

Fight the good fight, Paul.

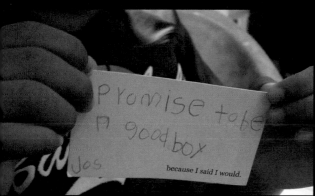

▲ **IN APRIL 2015,** I had a speaking engagement in the Philippines. While there, the host organization helped arrange a visit to the city of Tacloban, an area decimated by Super Typhoon Yolanda about eighteen months prior. At least 6,300 people died in the Philippines alone in this natural disaster. Even long after the typhoon, there were still buildings missing walls and roofs everywhere. I specifically remember seeing a giant ship that was sitting on dry land at least 300 yards from the shoreline. It had washed in during the storm and was now unmovable.

In Tacloban, I toured an orphanage where children had gone through unimaginable tragedy. Some of them were abandoned at hospitals because their families had been taken by the storm. Others where there for reasons disconnected from the typhoon; they had been turned over to the orphanage because they had been physically or sexually abused. I shared the idea of Promise Cards with them, and many of them began writing their own.

In all of this turmoil, the orphanage did not have a budget for a playground. While the kids deserve so much more, a lot of them just really wanted to a place to play. *Because I said I would* promised to provide the funding needed to make that happen. What once was an empty yard is now a place where kids can forget about the harshness of life, even if for just a moment.

The Quest of Two Sisters

Sam and Alex Buy a Van

You wouldn't be able to guess this by looking at her today, but Sam Kimura's nickname in high school was the Beast. You might think she looks like a model now, but in high school, Sam was a defensive powerhouse on her lacrosse team, destined for collegiate fields. Aggressive inline skating was another activity Sam loved growing up. She was considered a tomboy her whole life and wasn't afraid to take a hit.

Sam's sister, Alex, was quite the opposite. Older by two years and two months, she describes herself as a "super nerd." Today, Sam and Alex look remarkably alike, but Alex's interests have always been very different. Even as the older sister, Alex felt cool hanging out with Sam, who was undeniably one of the popular kids.

Sam (left) and Alex (right) Kimura

The Kimura sisters grew up in the '90s near Louisville, Kentucky, in a middle-class family. They enjoyed the kind of childhood you see in the movies, chasing each other around the neighborhood, hopping fences and jumping on trampolines.

Unlike most teenage siblings, Sam and Alex actually liked each other. Let me give you an example that illustrates this phenomenon. As little kids, they shared a room, but the day would come where they each could finally have a room of their own. They chose not to.

Late at night, their mom would constantly have to tell them to stop chatting.

"Go to sleep!" she would tell them.

Of course, they would just lower their voices. This interruption was simply an expected part of the routine. To end the night, the sisters would say the same jumbled sentence to each other.

"You love I Sam night," Alex would say. And then Sam would answer, "You love I Alex night." Played backward, that's "Night, Sam. I love you" and "Night, Alex. I love you."

In April 2010, when Sam was seventeen years old, she came down with a fever. Mrs. Kimura was anxious because her daughter was clearly very ill. Her fever was so intense she had to be checked in to the hospital. It was so bad, in fact, that Alex, who was a sophomore at Western Kentucky University, drove more than a hundred miles back home to see her sister.

Right at the moment Alex walked into Sam's hospital room for the first time, Sam's doctor walked in too. He explained to the two sisters and their mother that hospital testing revealed that Sam had severe aplastic anemia. The Kimura family had never heard of this disease. The doctor's high-level explanation, paired with his quick departure, left them in the dark. Not wanting to alarm her sister, Alex took a seat in the corner, flipped open her laptop and Googled *severe aplastic anemia*. The search results explained that if the disease goes untreated, the diagnosed can sometimes have only six months to live.

Big sisters are supposed to model strength, so Alex held herself together long enough to walk out into the hallway so that Sam wouldn't see her cry.

On the day she was diagnosed, Sam had only 10 percent of the bone marrow a healthy person should have. Because of this rare blood disorder, her bone marrow was not able to make enough blood cells for her body. The only cure for severe aplastic anemia is a bone marrow transplant (also called a stem cell transplant) to replace diseased cells with healthy ones. It is a long and complex process. First, the diseased bone marrow is reduced with radiation or chemotherapy. Then healthy stem cells are injected into the bloodstream. After the transplant, drugs are administered to help prevent rejection of the donated stem cells.

Finding a match is tremendously more complicated than finding a blood donor: Siblings have the highest possibility of being compatible, but even then it is only a one-in-four chance. Alex and other members of her family were tested the day of her diagnosis, and their samples were sent off to the lab. Sam immediately started on blood transfusions to buy her time until a donor could be found, and the family settled in to wait for the results.

Alex went back to Western Kentucky University. Her mom called her a week later. Reflecting back on the impact of that call, Alex said, "I have never had such a strong physical reaction to words. I dropped to my knees." Alex was not a match. Neither was anyone in their family.

A big sister or a big brother is supposed to be there for their younger siblings. That is what Alex believes. Her strong sense of duty is perhaps biologically ingrained in her. She felt it was her job to save her sister, and she felt like she had failed.

Sam's family learned more about this deadly disease as time progressed, and the reality hit home about how many people need bone marrow donors. Although severe aplastic anemia is very rare, in a single year, more than 17,000 people are diagnosed with a range of life-threatening illnesses where a bone marrow or umbilical cord blood transplant is their best treatment option. About 12,000 of them have to find a donor outside their family.[22]

Sam and her family started hosting events to sign people up for the registry of the National Marrow Donor Program. Signing up is a simple process: You just swab the inside of your cheek for saliva and mail it to the registry to see if you could be a life-saving match for someone in desperate need. They did this regularly for four years after Sam's diagnosis in 2010.

---

22 "Donor Information," Health Resources & Services Administration, Accessed on May 3, 2018. https://bloodcell.transplant.hrsa.gov/donor/index.html.

Meanwhile, Sam continued on an aggressive treatment program of multiple blood and platelet transfusions. To suppress her own immune system and prevent her body from attacking itself, Sam had to take more than twenty medications daily.

In the spring of 2014, Sam and Alex were eating dinner at an Olive Garden, talking about what was next in their lives. At age twenty-one and twenty-three, they were tossing around ideas for something bigger they could do to help grow the National Marrow Donor Program. One of the two sisters said something that would change their lives forever: "What if we went to all fifty states?" To this day, the Kimura sisters still say that the best ideas come from breadsticks.

So, that's what they promised. The plan was to set up tables to sign people up for the National Marrow Donor Program registry in each one of the fifty states. Alex was so dedicated to this plan that she quit her job at the Livestrong Foundation (a nonprofit cancer support organization) in Austin, Texas. Sam was a junior in college at the time and dropped out to devote herself to the cause. Their good friend, Taylor Shorten, also joined them. Sam and Alex decided to sell their cars in order to buy a van the three girls could live in during the journey. Their pushpin roadmap targeted colleges, because research suggests that young adult donors provide more and better bone marrow cells.[23]

Their journey began on January 20, 2015, in Louisville, Kentucky. It was a true adventure. The three young women got to see America in a way that most people never will, taking in the bustling nature of our cities, the lonely stretches of highway, the beautiful rolling hills, and the mountains and rivers. But it also came with a lot of rejection. Students can sometimes be immature, and many people believe that marrow donation is difficult

---

23 "Why a donor's age matters," Be the Match, National Marrow Donor Program, Accessed on May 3, 2018, https://bethematch.org/transplant-basics/matching-patients-with-donors/why-donor-age-matters/.

David Harris, "Opinion: Younger is Better," *The Scientist*, August 12, 2012, https://www.the-scientist.com/?articles.view/articleNo/32483/title/Opinion--Younger-Is-Better/.

or painful. At the registration table, they may laugh at you, ignore you, or give you a flat-out no.

For Alex, that was the hardest part: telling the story of Sam and the life-threatening nature of her disease. With Sam standing right there, strangers would reply to her face, "No, that's not something I would want to do." To Alex, they might as well be saying, "Your sister is dying, and I don't care enough to do anything about it."

But that didn't stop them. In their trip to all fifty states, Sam, Alex, and Taylor signed up over 24,000 potential donors, and they discovered thirty-three DNA matches that have led to five possible life-saving donations for adults and children in desperate need.

On the last bit of their journey, they had to ditch their van, which had accrued more than 20,000 miles on the trip. The adventure ended in Hawaii on December 15, 2015. Sam and Alex fulfilled their promise. They saved the lives of strangers, and they brought national attention to an important cause. But there was still no match for Sam. That doesn't shake their commitment, though, and they are still advocating for the National Marrow Donor Program to this day.

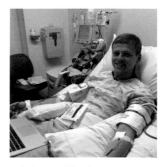

A donor giving bone marrow

There are probably a lot of things that we could learn from Alex and Sam's journey, but one thing I take from all this is something we haven't talked about much at all—the impact of Taylor Shorten, their friend who joined them from the very beginning. *The Quest of Two Sisters* is a catchy title but leaves out an important truth. The truth is that often behind a great promise kept, there is someone who goes unnoticed, an unknown hero that the promise always needed. This promise needed Taylor from the very beginning, but there is still another hero remaining out there who will hopefully help end this story the right way. The hero that swabs their cheek and becomes Sam's only match. Is it you? There is only one want to find out. Go to DKMS.org and request your swabbing kit. ■

Taylor (left), Alex (middle), and Sam (right)

Row, Row, Row

Wisdom from Katie Spotz

Katie Spotz joined the *because I said I would* staff in January 2016 to help support the growth of our chapter program. Among all our conversations at work, there's one quote of Katie's that stands out: "It's okay to think you can't do it, but that doesn't mean you're right." That quote means a lot coming from her, because Katie Spotz is the youngest person in the world to row a boat across the Atlantic Ocean solo.

When I say row, I mean like "row, row, row your boat, gently down the stream" kind of row. But instead of a stream it's a 2,817-mile stretch of the Atlantic Ocean. In 2010, at age twenty-two, Katie spent seventy days alone at sea in a bright-yellow ocean rowboat without any rescue support. She successfully crossed the Atlantic Ocean and fulfilled her promise in order to raise awareness about the global water crisis, because every twenty seconds, somewhere in the world a child dies from lack of access to clean drinking water.[24] Katie supports a nonprofit

---

24 Steve Contorno, "Matt Damon: 'Every 20 seconds, a child dies because they lack access to clean water and sanitation,'" PunditFact, March 23, 2014, http://www.politifact.com/punditfact/statements/2014/mar/23/matt-damon/matt-damon-every-20-seconds-child-dies-because-the/.

"The Water Crisis," Water.org, Accessed on May 4, 2018, https://water.org/our-impact/water-crisis/.

called H2O for Life, which provides service-learning opportunities in schools, helping teachers and students get involved in bringing water to the developing world.

As if conquering an ocean wasn't enough, Katie has also swum all 325 miles of the Allegheny River; she's the first person ever to accomplish that. Katie rode a bicycle across the United States—twice. On the second crossing, she broke her pelvis in a bicycle crash and completed the journey on a hand bike. To top it all off, when I was writing this book, I talked to her on the phone, and she was preparing to complete a 100-mile run in under twenty-four hours of total time.

Even the way Katie trains seems superhuman. When she runs on a treadmill at the gym, instead of counting the miles or minutes, Katie sometimes challenges herself in a different way. She starts running, and she won't get off her treadmill until ten other people get off their treadmills. What if there were only nine people on treadmills at the gym, though? Katie would keep running, waiting for some stranger to eventually arrive at the gym, park their car, change in the locker room, find a treadmill, start running, and stop running before she would get off. I once walked across the state of Ohio in ten days for a humanitarian cause, but I don't like to bring that up when Katie is around. She could do something like that on a whim if she felt like there wasn't anything good on TV.

But in the break room, she microwaves her mac and cheese just like everyone else. It might be some sort of protein-boosted quinoa pasta, but you get what I'm trying to say. Outside of physically being some sort of superhero, she is really a human being like the rest of us, and she has challenges like anyone else.

After she gives a speech about her adventures, during the question-and-answer session, people often ask her things like, "Isn't it lonely out on that boat by yourself?" Her knee-jerk response is, "No. It was okay." But that isn't entirely what she means. You see, she did feel lonely on that boat, but she answers like that because she has always felt alone.

"I'm okay with saying that I felt very alone in my upbringing. I was so used to feeling alone," Katie says. When she was growing up, there was turbulence between her parents, and Katie felt isolated. These days, she

conquers loneliness by taking her own advice: "It's okay to think you can't do it, but that doesn't mean you're right."

Katie works at a new place now, but she participates in one of our local chapters. She likes to be prepared and so do we; most recently, she joined our chapter's promise to help others become CPR certified. Katie is studying to become a certified personal trainer. It seems to me that setting a world record for rowing across the Atlantic Ocean should automatically come with some sort of certification, but then again, I'm not in charge of those kinds of things.

I like it when amazing people seem so normal when you get to know them. It makes me feel like we're all not far from being incredible. "It's okay to think you can't do it, but that doesn't mean you're right." I know I've written that three times now, but it bears repeating. ■

A Six-Year-Old's Handwriting

The Determination of Eugene Lim

I n 2010, six-year-old Eugene Lim was sitting at a table in his home in a Chicago suburb, writing a letter. *Dear Eugene*, he began. Eugene was writing to himself in the future. He was congratulating himself on achieving the rank of Eagle Scout, the highest honor a Boy Scout can achieve.

Writing always came easier to Eugene than speaking. He was born with a speech impediment, and he didn't talk until he was three years old. His stutter has never affected his intelligence or his ability to learn, though. In fact, it was clear early on that Eugene was a gifted child. Although his speech was delayed, he could communicate his understanding of the alphabet before the age of two. Eugene went on to join Mensa (a society of people with IQ scores in the top 2 percent of the population) at age nine and became a member of its Junior Honor Society at age ten.

Along with this intelligence, Eugene's interest in community service also started at a young age. Independent volunteering is sometimes a requirement of youth development programs. "The thing is," he explains, "not many places allow ten-year-olds to volunteer." After many hours of researching nonprofits, making phone calls, and meeting

Eugene in the fifth grade

Eugene and his family

dead ends, Eugene and his parents spoke to the organizers at the local food bank, who agreed to let him volunteer. "My first shift at the food bank was on July 1, 2014, scooping granola cereal into bags. In two hours, our group of about ten people produced 968 meals," Eugene explains. "At this pace, I am humbled to know that [in a year's time] over 50,000 people will not go hungry."

Before the age of thirteen, Eugene Lim had volunteered more than 167 hours at the food bank. For his inspirational service, in 2015, the food bank named Eugene Lim their Youth Volunteer of the Year. Chicago's *Daily Herald* ran an article about him, including a photo showing him wearing one of his favorite shirts, which happened to say *because I said I would.*

Part of Eugene's passion for integrity and service come from his love of the Boy Scouts. It's something that must run in the family: His grandpa was a member of the Boy Scouts in Malaysia, and so was his dad. When his dad moved to Eugene, Oregon (after which Eugene is named), he continued in Boy Scouts there, as well. While Scouting is a strong legacy in the family, no one had ever achieved the Eagle Scout rank.

Becoming an Eagle Scout is very difficult to achieve, which is part of what makes it such an admirable ambition. Even for someone like Eugene, who knows all about hard work, Eagle Scout is still a stretch. Only one in twenty Boy Scouts ever completes all of the rigorous requirements in the areas of leadership, service, and outdoor skills that are necessary for the Eagle Scout rank. Not only that, the clock is ticking. The cutoff age to become an Eagle Scout is eighteen. Most people manage to complete the requirements just in time to beat the cutoff age: In 2015, the average age for becoming an Eagle Scout was seventeen.[25] Eugene Lim achieved the Eagle Scout ranking when he was only twelve years old.

Some of the other boys in Eugene's troop are sixteen or seventeen years old now, and they are also striving for their Eagle Scout ranking. At the Court of Honor, where he was awarded Scouting's highest rank, Eugene read out the letter that he wrote to himself when he was just six years old and assured his fellow scouts that they too could reach their goal. Eugene even handed out Promise Cards to everyone, encouraging them to make the same commitment he made to himself.

In the normal course of events, Eugene would be moving into eighth grade at the time of this writing. However, because of his remarkable aca-

demic achievements, he is moving straight into his sophomore year in high school. Ultimately, he aims to go to college and become an aeronautical engineer. If there are any astronauts out there reading this, it would be awesome if you wrote a letter to Eugene. Instead of retreating into self-pity over his stutter or isolating himself in the studies in which he excelled, this young boy pushes his comfort zone in order to help others in need.

It is incredibly important that we teach our children subjects like math, science, reading, and

25 Bryan Wendell, "This is how the average age of Eagle Scouts in 2017 compared to previous years," ScoutingMagazine.org, February 22, 2018, https://blog.scoutingmagazine.org/2018/02/22/average-age-eagle-scouts-dipped-slightly-2017/.

writing. Academics are critical, but at the same time, if we do not teach our children how to be decent human beings to one another, then what is the point of society at all? That is why *because I said I would* heavily invests in character education—the opportunity to teach children concepts like honesty, self-control, and accountability in the classroom. That is why we provide lesson plans at no cost to educators, that is why we have student chapters of *because I said I would*, and that is why I visited Eugene's school for an assembly speech when he was nine. I didn't know who he was that day, but I surely know who he is now. ■

Surfing in Lake Michigan

Dave Benjamin Is a Little Crazy

In 1987, twelve-year-old Dave Benjamin was sitting in a movie theater just outside of Chicago, Illinois, watching a movie called *North Shore*. It's kind of like *The Karate Kid*, but with surfboards. A surf gang robs the teenage main character, and a mystic, a Mr. Miyagi–type board-shaping master takes him as an apprentice. Today, it would be considered an over-the-top eighties movie, but when little Dave was watching it for the first time in the theater, he was wide eyed and captivated by the sport of surfing. Dave grew up with that movie playing in the back of his mind, but Chicago wasn't exactly the best place to catch waves.

When Dave was in his early twenties, he was driving home through a Midwestern snowstorm one day when he saw something that didn't make sense to him. He saw an old station wagon with a surfboard on its roof, and on the bumper of the station wagon, there was sticker that read, *Third Coast Surf Shop*.

This is crazy, he thought. *What is this person doing?*

Later, Dave got on his computer and discovered that Third Coast Surf Shop was a real surf shop—in New Buffalo, Michigan? They sold surfboards, wet suits, boots, gloves—all the equipment that you might need to surf *in the Great Lakes*. By a strange twist of fate, Dave was going to be working near New Buffalo for the next couple of weeks.

He started researching surfing the Great Lakes through online forums. He didn't want to visit the surf shop and embarrass himself with newbie questions. He remembered something like that happening in the movie.

Having equipped himself with what he thought was just enough knowledge, when he got to New Buffalo, he walked into the surf shop and asked to try on a wet suit. In the changing room, the elastic wet suit got stuck on him and he couldn't get it off. After struggling with this python for an unreasonable amount of time, he eventually gave up, waddled out in defeat, and asked for help. But embarrassment wasn't enough to stop Dave Benjamin that day. He bought what he needed, said thank you, and left.

Surfing the Great Lakes has many challenges. The cold is an obvious one, but just like the gangs in *North Shore*, the local surfers are a little territorial. They weren't really forthcoming with telling Dave where to go surfing, but they did let slip that the best time to go surfing is in the fall and the winter. This is when the best wind-producing weather patterns form. However, the water might be an icy thirty-two degrees—and treacherous. Ice floes, forbidding currents, and enormous waves can make for dangerous conditions, as Dave learned firsthand.

Ten years after that first purchase, Dave could now call other surfers newbies. On December 26, 2010, Dave was tracking a weather pattern that would end up changing his life. He was messaging back and forth with his buddies. "Are we going to do this? Are the conditions right?"

They were.

Dave got in his truck and headed to the beach, where the winter air was coming down from the lake. It was maybe twenty degrees colder at the beach than it was inland. The confines of his truck cabin made it difficult, but Dave managed to squeeze himself into his wet suit, boots, gloves, and hood.

You would think it would be absolutely freezing out there in that lake water, but Dave assured me it's not. "When you first step in, that first bit of water that seeps

Dave covered in ice

into the suit is pretty cold. But once you get a little water in, it seals up. Then your body warms the water as you paddle. In the winter, you don't want to take a break on the beach; you simply surf pretty much to exhaustion. You try to keep your body warm through movement, and who knows when the weather will break. The fatigue is blended with elation, though. After a chess game of patience and positioning, you find yourself in just the right spot to turn and paddle before the wave's momentum takes you, lifting your board up. You get on your feet, fall into a bottom turn—a traditional move using your weight and balance to turn into the wave—and then take the clean space of the wave to carve down the line." Dave tried to paint a picture for me, but words are not enough. He ended by saying simply, "It's full exhilaration, man. That's what's going on."

On that particular day in December, Dave caught as many waves as he could. As the ice floes started to come into the lineup where the waves were breaking, he told himself, *I'll hit one last wave and then I'll go in.*

Then he looked over his shoulder.

Dave saw a big wave peaking up unexpectedly close behind him. He committed, but it was too late: The wave was already curving overhead. It caught him and catapulted him upward. He landed flat on his back. In the next moment, another wave crashed down on him, water pounding his face. The frigid water coursed through the suit's opening on his face, flushing his body with freezing temperatures and pushing him to the depths.

Struggling to breathe, the force of the water holding him under, Dave realized that his surfboard leash was not tugging at his ankle. His board was his flotation device, and that security blanket was gone. Dave clawed his way to the surface and was just about to take a breath when another wave forced him under once more. Despite all his years of swimming, panic quickly became terror. When he finally made it to the surface once more, Dave tried to wave to his buddies, but they were two hundred yards away. They couldn't see his gestures for help and to make things worse, holding his hands above his head made Dave sink again.

"I was holding my last breath and thinking, *I'm not going home. This is it.* Someone's going to be knocking at the door to tell my parents, my children, and my wife that I died surfing in Lake Michigan."

His body stopped fighting.

But his mind was still moving. In this moment, Dave's tired brain recalled an article he read on Third Coast Surf Shop's website. It was called "Drowning Doesn't Look Like Drowning."[26] The article listed all the signs of drowning: facing shore, mouth at water level, head tilted back, hyperventilating, and the "climbing the ladder" motion. And Dave realized he was doing all these things.

"The more I'm struggling to stay above water, the more I'm sinking and dying. Maybe if I stop doing this, I'll be okay," he told me, recalling the moment.

With his last bit of strength, Dave applied the "flip, float, and follow" strategy defined in that article. Flip over on your back, then float to keep your head above water, and conserve your energy. Then while you're floating, follow (don't fight) the current and find the safest course back to dry land. "I realized I could survive. I could float. I could stay at the surface," Dave says.

But Dave's problems were not over. The waves were pushing him toward the jagged rocks of the shore. This cliff edge was fifteen feet high, and if he hit it he might not survive. When he got close to the wall, he felt a countercurrent pulling him further out, away from the rock wall—but of course, also away from shore.

The cycle of these circling currents continued for forty minutes. In the fight of his life, Dave eventually made it to shore safely. As Dave crawled out of the icy lake—battered, exhausted, bone weary—he made a promise to himself: "I decided that I was going to do everything I could to promote water safety, drowning prevention, and rip-current awareness."

Dave's damaged surfboard in the water

Did you know that more school-aged children die by drowning in the

---

26   Mario Vittone, "Drowning Doesn't Look Like Drowning," Mario Vittone, May 3, 2010. http://mariovittone.com/2010/05/154/.

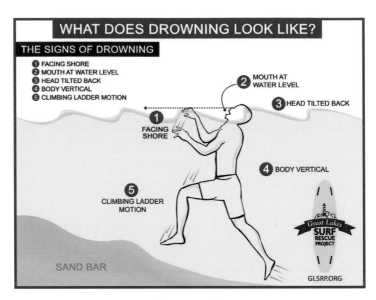

WHAT DOES DROWNING LOOK LIKE?

THE SIGNS OF DROWNING

1. FACING SHORE
2. MOUTH AT WATER LEVEL
3. HEAD TILTED BACK
4. BODY VERTICAL
5. CLIMBING LADDER MOTION

2. MOUTH AT WATER LEVEL

3. HEAD TILTED BACK

1. FACING SHORE

4. BODY VERTICAL

5. CLIMBING LADDER MOTION

SAND BAR

GLSRP.ORG

Great Lakes SURF RESCUE PROJECT

http://greatlakeswatersafety.org/tips/

United States each year than by fires, tornadoes, active shooters, earthquakes, and lightning combined?[27] The World Health Organization and Center for Disease Control statistics show that to be true.[28] It seems strange that when you ask any kid, "What do you do if you're on fire?" basically everyone replies with stop, drop, and roll. But when you ask children, "What do you do when you are drowning?" you get blank stares. Most people don't know because there is so little water-safety education in school.

After his experiences that winter day, Dave decided to start a community project to help young children understand water safety. He joined forces with the Great Lakes Surf Rescue Project, a nonprofit whose mission is to be a leader in water safety and reduce the number of drownings through training, public preparedness, and public awareness. Dave eventually became the executive director of public relations and project management for that

27 Javonte Anderson, "Water safety training comes to Lake Michigan," *Post Tribune*, June 6, 2016, http://www.chicagotribune.com/suburbs/post-tribune/news/ct-ptb-rescue-training-st-0607-20160606-story.html.

28 "Global Report on Drowning: Preventing a Leading Killer," World Health Organization, 2014, http://www.who.int/violence_injury_prevention/publications/drowning_global_report/Final_report_full_web.pdf.

organization, where he presents water-safety classes in seven of the eight Great Lakes states.

"The longer you're floating, the longer you're alive," Dave explained to me. "What we know about drowning is that time is of the essence. Once you are submerged, you have fewer than sixty seconds. At two minutes of submersion, if artificial respiration is properly performed, there's a 92 percent chance of survival. At ten minutes of submersion, there's a 14 percent survival. After ten minutes of submersion, unfortunately, it's a recovery effort. If you can float two minutes, five minutes, ten minutes, you're buying the time you need to survive. There have been instances where people have floated for as long as thirty-six hours. If you don't know how to float, start practicing your floating skills today. Learn the signs of drowning: facing shore, mouth at water level, head tilted back, and climbing the ladder."

Each year, Dave Benjamin fulfills his promise to help children understand the dangers of open water by speaking at school assemblies. But it doesn't really matter where you ask him to go. He will meet a bunch of adults at a bar for a scuba club meeting, he will speak to a Boy Scouts Troop or even present at a homeowners' association if that's what it takes. Even if only a handful of people will be there to listen, Dave Benjamin still shows up.

Between March and June 2016, Dave conducted about two hundred water-safety presentations. He gets a small daily stipend from the nonprofit, but it's not enough to make a living. To pay the bills, Dave works as a residential painter. His passion does not come without sacrifice. "I survived a drowning accident, and since then, I've been drowning financially to advocate for water safety."

I will dedicate my life to Water safety and create a Water Safety School curriculum — **because I said I would.**

That is not fair. But unfortunately, life is not fair. If you're feeling bad for Dave Benjamin right now, remember that many people will live their entire lives not understanding their purpose. For all the things Dave doesn't have, at least he has that: a purpose. ■

Sacrifice

AN UNFORTUNATE REALITY

....

When I was growing up, there was a saying my mom often repeated to me with a loving smile: "Whoever told you life was fair lied to you." As a child, I took this as part of the standard script that all moms must administer, but with time, I came to see its broader truth. She was trying to help me understand that hardships are a part of existence. If you want something bad enough, you're going to have to sacrifice to get it. It seems that every new generation takes one step further away from this understanding. Maybe that's because many things are now done for us with just the touch of a screen. We quickly forget that other parts of life will never work that way.

We fight ourselves over the fairness or convenience of obligations. People waste a lot of valuable energy in an unproductive internal dialogue protesting the discomfort of their commitments:

I don't want to wake up. It's too early.
Can't he do this himself? Why do I need to go?
I shouldn't have agreed to this.

Yet someone who is elite in commitment has learned to avoid this pointless routine.

The elite have developed what we call *promise acceptance*. Promise acceptance is when a person no longer argues with themselves about the realities of a promise they already know they are going to keep. The mantra?

"It is what it is."

You can see promise acceptance in many of the stories in this book. The girl who testified against her rapist understood that if she was going to save the next person from becoming a victim, she had to sit in the witness stand whether she liked it or not. Alex Kimura knew that she had to quit her job to help her sister, Sam, search for a bone marrow donor match, even if success wasn't guaranteed. Eventually, a day comes where the argument ends and you just say to yourself, "It doesn't matter if this is fair. I'm doing it anyway, so what's the point in fighting it anymore? Complaining isn't accomplishing anything and I have a promise to keep."

With genuine promise acceptance, a dramatic shift is possible. When we stop the banter, we open up new mental space that we can use to plan, prepare, and problem solve. It's easier to focus when you're staring down only one road

Even though the word *sacrifice* sounds so serious, thankfully there is a bright side to it. Somewhere in human nature our biology gives a reward for what we give up for others. The idea of a "warm and fuzzy" feeling that comes after you accomplish an act of kindness is real. Even very young children experience it: In 2012, a Canadian study found that before the age of two, toddlers exhibit greater happiness when giving treats to others than receiving treats themselves. Perhaps most striking is that children were happier when they engaged in giving up their own resources than when giving resources at no cost to themselves.[29]

Some may criticize people who get even a little happiness from the sacrifices they make for others. They may have more concern for a literal definition of altruism than an actual commitment to sacrifice. Critics may claim that a teacher working for underserved children for an inadequate salary is paid in the satisfaction they have in changing lives. Many mistakenly put equal weight on both sacrifice and sense of purpose and forget how hard it is to do the right thing even if it's the right thing.

We should be proud of the sacrifices we make for others. In reality, there isn't always a great deal of reward outside of that warm feeling—embrace it. You gave up something. You could have done something self-serving with your time, your talents, or your

29 Aknin, L., Broesch, T., Hamlin, J.K., and Van de Vondervoot, J. W., "Prosocial Behavior Leads to Happiness in a Small-Scale Rural Society," *Journal of Experimental Psychology: General*, 144: 4, 788-795, 2015, https://www.broeschlab.ca/wp-content/uploads/2017/10/Aknin-et-al.-2015-Prosocial-Behavior-Leads-to-Happiness-in-a-Small-Scale-Rural-Society.pdf

oney, but you didn't. Instead, you chose to believe in somethin
igger. Hang on to that joy because another sacrifice may com
d you are going to have to convince yourself of why you need t
crifice again. ■

Sacrifice

—

It is an unfortunate reality that the betterment of humanity requires sacrifice. Voluntarily giving away what we cherish, even if for a greater cause, is difficult. I accept that life is not easy. Decisions must be made, and so must sacrifices as well.

because I said I would.

because I said I would.

253

▲ **"ON SEPTEMBER 10, 1996,** my father hung himself in our garage. (My mother and I found him on our way home from school.) From that day forward, my mom, my supermom, gave up her entire life to care for me on a private school elementary teacher's salary. She has selflessly provided for me in ways that make me question her humanity. Surely no mortal could prepare chocolate chip pancakes or omelets for breakfast every morning, cart a selfish child to and from dance practice, soccer, swimming, and piano, send that same child to a private college and graduate school . . . and manage to work sixty hours a week for over a decade?!

"That amazing woman is still working herself to death because she cannot afford to retire, which breaks my heart. I promise to provide for her in every way I possibly can—as she has for me—for the rest of our days. We may be separated by distance, but I will work every day to be able to make my way back to her and give her half of the joy, love, respect, and wisdom she extended to me throughout my childhood and now . . . because, as she loves to say, 'We're all each other has!'"

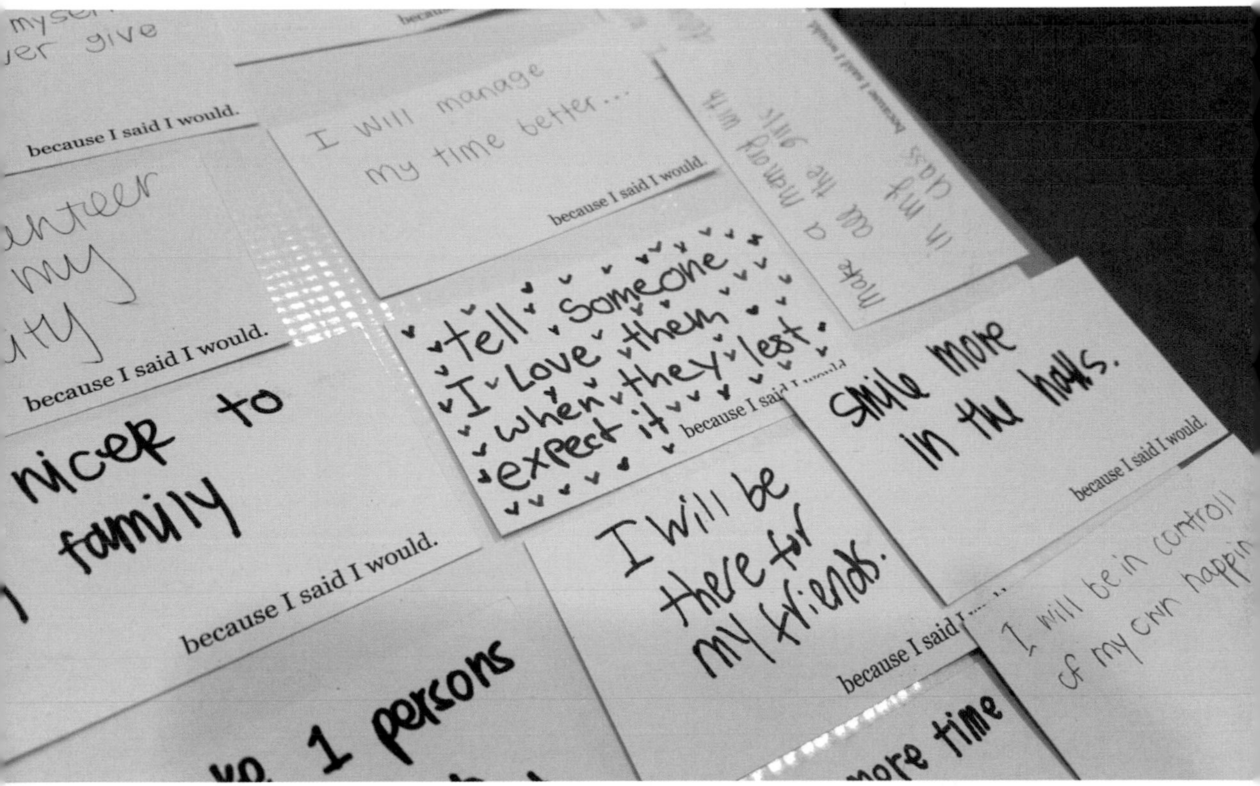

myse...
...er give

because I said I would.

...nteer
my
...ty

because I said I would.

nicer to
family

because I said I would.

...e 1 persons

I will manage
my time better...

because I said I would.

bec...

tell someone
I love them
when they lest
expect it

because I said I would.

I will be
there for
my friends.

because I said I...

more time

...will...
make a manage with
in my class
with all the girls

smile more
in the halls.

because I said I would.

I will be in controll
of my own happin...

Let go of regret
you're doing the
best you can !

because I said I would.

▲ **SOMETIMES THE VICTIMS** of sex trafficking are only alone when they have to "wash up" right before they are abused. In an attempt to reach these individuals, chapter members of *because I said I would,* Cleveland, held a meeting to label 5,000 bars of hotel soap with the phone number of the National Human Trafficking Resource Center. We partnered with S.O.A.P., a nonprofit in Ohio that helps put a stop to human trafficking and save missing children, to help understand the issue and be a small part of the solution.

In memory of Vincent Canzani

▲ **SEVENTEEN MEMBERS FROM** the *because I said I would* chapter in Akron, Ohio, showed up to plant trees in memory of someone who is no longer with us. We recorded the exact GPS coordinates of each tree. People handle death in different ways. Sometimes you just want something to go back to.

Sometime after this charitable promise, membership across all our adult chapters began to decline. We doubled down on the program by hiring more staff, increasing marketing efforts, and making changes to hopefully increase the appeal of volunteering with us. Unfortunately, 75.1 percent of Americans do not volunteer even a single time in an entire year*, so recruiting volunteers is an uphill battle.

After months of continued efforts, the decline in membership continued. Ultimately, we had to come to the decision to close our three adult chapters and reallocate those resources to *because I said I would* high school chapters, which have a much higher participation rate. It is every nonprofit's responsibility to build efficient and cost-effective programs. When we fall short of this obligation, we must hold ourselves accountable even if that means pausing a program. But in the words of F. Scott Fitzgerald . . .
"Never confuse a single defeat with a final defeat."

Our high school chapters are growing in numbers. We aim to start middle school and college chapters one day. We even hope that this book might build a wave of support to restart the adult chapters program. If everything in our journey were an instant success, then our movement wouldn't truly know what commitment is really like. We just have to do what our supporters do. Keep trying.

I will
be on time

because I said I would.

I will never break
my wedding vows
to Paul.
because I said I would.

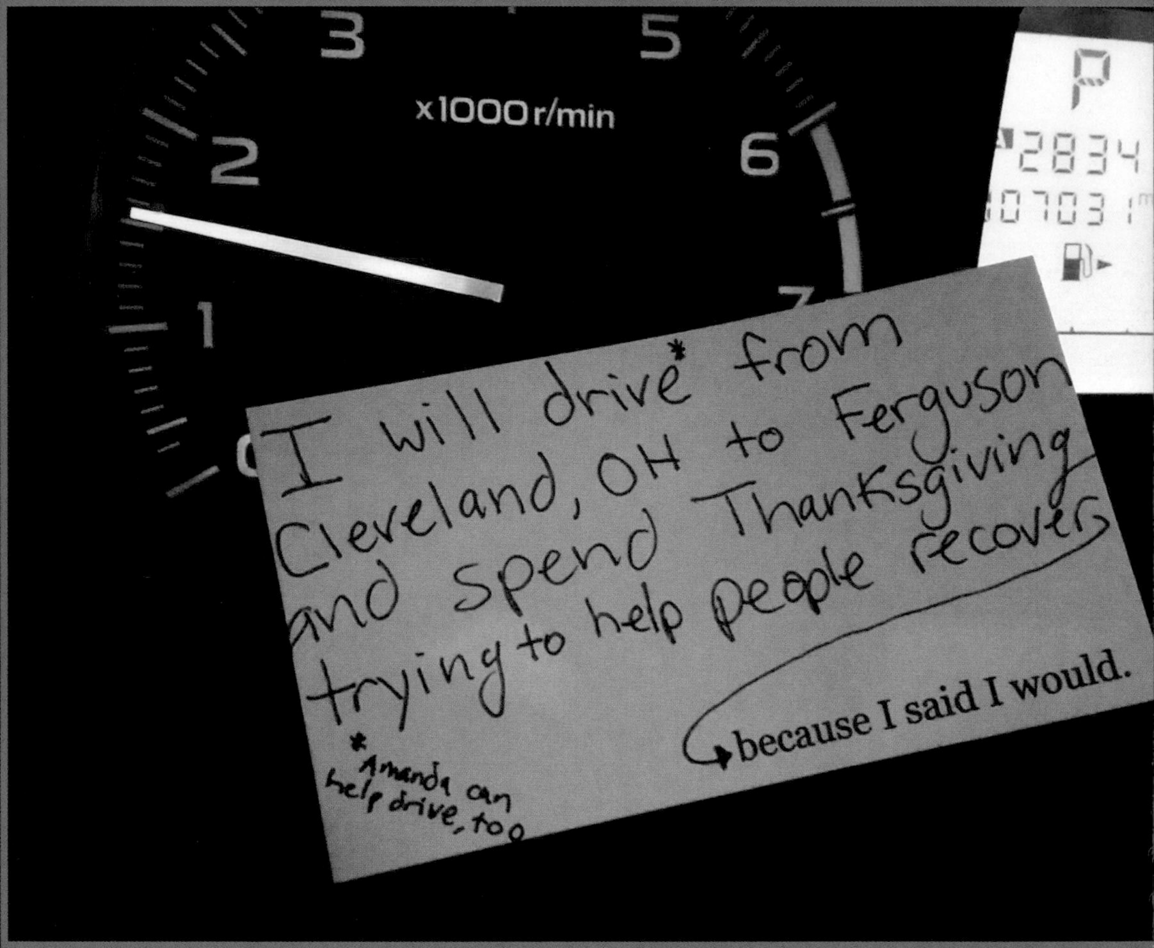
3
5
x1000 r/min
2
6
1
P
2834
07031
I will drive* from
Cleveland, OH to Ferguson
and spend Thanksgiving
trying to help people recover
because I said I would.
*Amanda can
help drive, too

▲ **HELPING BEAUTIFY**
Ferguson, Missouri
after rioters broke
into businesses

The Big Porch Upstairs

Erin Comes Up Short

In October 2013, in Lakewood, Ohio, Erin Huber, age thirty-one, was sitting on the large upstairs porch of the duplex she lived in, overlooking the steady movement of cars down Clifton Boulevard. She was alone, and she was crying.

Erin was leaving the next day for Uganda. She was the founder of a new nonprofit called Drink Local. Drink Tap., a nonprofit dedicated to clean-water initiatives. She was not crying because this is her first trip to Africa—in fact, she'd been there many times before. It was not a matter of fear. She was crying because she wasn't able to reach the fundraising goal that would have covered a second phase of the drinking water project that she was flying out for—a tapped clean water system for a village in desperate need of clean water. Erin had put countless unpaid hours into making this happen.

"I had worked so hard to plan this project, to get everything in line," she told me. "All the people, all the materials, so many fundraisers—I'd poured my heart and soul into the project, and I hadn't gotten that big hit that we needed." Even though the first phase of the project—installing a well to bring drinking water to this particular village—had been completed successfully, she couldn't help but think of the consequences of her shortfall. The failure to find the funding for the second part of the project had life-and-death implications for children.

According to the World Health Organization, diarrheal disease is the second leading cause of death in children under five years old.[30] This is both preventable and treatable, because a significant proportion of diarrheal disease can be avoided through safe drinking water and the hygiene practices that can come with it.

As Erin sat outside on her porch, Erin's roommate looked through the window and could see her tears. When you live with someone who is committed to a cause, you know that this kind of emotion isn't for attention. People like Erin don't need to be standing in front of suffering to feel that it is there. One mile away or ten thousand miles away—to her, a life is a life.

Erin's roommate opened the door to the porch and walked over to console her friend. In her roommate's hand was a two-page handwritten note. This letter was a testimony to Erin's commitment and love she has for others in need. It was witness to the hard work that Erin's roommate knew went into this project. She handed Erin the handwritten note as a reminder that there were people out there who knew she did the best she could. Along with this letter, Erin's roommate also handed her a check for $10,000. It was a large portion of the funding necessary to complete the second phase of the water project in Uganda.

And who was Erin's roommate?

---

30 "Diarrhoeal disease," World Health Organization, May 2, 2017, http://www.who.int/en/news-room/fact-sheets/detail/diarrhoeal-disease.

Erin Huber's roommate happened to be Katie Spotz, the youngest woman in the world to row a boat across the Atlantic Ocean. Katie wanted her success as a world-renowned ultra-athlete to mean success for others in need. She was confident that Erin would steward these funds honorably.

Because of Katie's help, Erin's project was a complete success.

That was five years ago. Today, in 2018, Erin has become an expert in clean water. If you don't stop her, she will ramble on about drilling boreholes and other engineering terms I don't completely understand. Erin often leaves her home in Cleveland, Ohio, for months at a time to directly manage these construction projects in Ugandan villages.

Erin at a clean water construction site in Uganda

Along the way Erin has learned a lot of hard lessons on what it takes to create a successful clean-water project. It is an unfortunate reality that more than half of clean-water projects fail.[31] Water wells require regular maintenance and unique repairs. Unless a project is managed sustainably, a village will soon find itself back in its original turmoil. In the six years that Erin has been doing her work in Africa, 100 percent of Drink Local. Drink Tap. installations are still fully functional at the time of this writing.

I asked Erin what her advice would be for people who aspire to start a nonprofit.

"Don't," she said with a chuckle.

We both laughed because of our shared individual experiences as

---

31   John James, " Sanitizing the Truth—When Wash Fails," Irin, https://www.irinnews.org/analysis/2013/09/17/sanitizing-truth-when-wash-fails.

nonprofit leaders and the hardships that have come with the job. But she went on to explain that there are a lot of worthy causes already out there to support—organizations that have already learned the hard lessons, that are running efficiently and are desperate to recruit hardworking people who want to make an impact through their existing infrastructure. But if you are one of those people hell-bent on starting your own nonprofit, take this advice: Volunteer or work at other nonprofits to learn from their successes and mistakes. This background can prepare you for the challenges of fundraising, teach you how to develop a theory of change, or show you how to measure meaningful outcomes. Helping people is harder than it sounds. Equip yourself with knowledge before you make the leap. You're going to need it. ■

▲ "I promise to build five more water projects in Uganda this year."

The Casino Lobby

Lisa Decides to Go Big

Te best place for this story to happen is where it happened: Las Vegas, Nevada. In 2016, a business conference asked me to come speak at their event, which was being hosted at the Bellagio hotel. These moments often feel a bit uncomfortable for me. There is an obvious disparity between the excessive nature of the venue and the work of a small nonprofit. At these conferences, no matter the venue or the

audience, I don't tell people to make promises to sell more widgets, and we refuse to promote commercial activity. That isn't what we are about. Organizations that bring us in understand and respect our focus on personal and humanitarian promises.

On this day, I gave a speech as I often do. I waved to the audience as I finished and stepped through the curtains into the backstage area. I walked into a service hallway that emptied out into the public hallways, where audience members entered and left. Everyone was still in the session listening to the next speaker; the hallways were deserted.

Deserted, that is, except for two women. One was a blonde in her forties, and the other woman looked about old enough to be her mom, which in fact was the case. The younger woman stopped me. "Hi, I'm Lisa," she said.

We shook hands and chatted a little, but her name didn't ring a bell. I thought she was just someone who watched the speech and then came out to say hello. I had stepped off the stage maybe thirty seconds before seeing

these two women, so I was perhaps a little disoriented. I forgot that I actually knew who this woman was. I had never seen her face before because we had only spoken on the phone. Luckily, through our conversation, I realized who she was. Lisa was a very generous donor to our cause and had been invited by my assistant, Julie, to see me speak for the first time and eat lunch with me.

I was staying at a hotel close by, so I told Lisa and her mom that I just needed to grab my stuff from the room, and then I would meet them back at the Bellagio. I raced back to my hotel and packed everything at double speed. I have a place in my bag for each item. When I'm in a rush, I pat each pocket and ensure it's filled to the adequate level. If an area doesn't feel full enough, I audit that compartment. Everything in my bag felt right, so I looked around the room one last time just in case, and then I caught the elevator down to the ground level.

When I got back to the Bellagio, Lisa was standing in the lobby with her mom. As I approached her, she started talking.

"Alex, I was going to give this to you." She handed me an envelope. "It's a donation, but I've decided that it is not enough."

Lisa explained to me that she had recently gone through a divorce and that as a part of this life transition she was trying to decide what to do with her wedding ring. She had taken the diamond out of its setting, and she was debating whether she should sell it or if she should reset it in a new ring. She was really wrestling with the question of what this diamond should represent, now that her relationship was over. After all this deliberation, Lisa told me that the speech convinced her to do something else with the diamond. She decided that the diamond would serve a better purpose being donated to our charity.

I don't know much about diamonds, but you don't need to be a gemologist to be shocked by what Lisa said next: "The diamond is 5.56 karats. It is worth about $150,000."

I didn't understand what was happening in that moment. No one had ever given us any sort of donation even remotely close to this amount. Nonprofit leaders shouldn't need money to validate the importance of their work, but if you struggle with fundraising enough, you know that's easier said than felt. A donation feels like a literal vote of confidence for you and the cause you are fighting for. Right or wrong, you feel less alone. Nonprofit leaders often have to sacrifice a lot and when someone gives to your effort, it's like they're saying, "I will sacrifice with you."

In that hotel lobby, I gave Lisa and her mom a warm hug. Then we went to lunch on time, just as the schedule stated. After lunch, Lisa took me to the jeweler where the diamond was stored for cleaning. She didn't want to ship the diamond to me; she was going to physically hand it to me. Lisa parked her car in front of the jeweler and went inside. I sat and chatted with her mom. Not more than ten minutes later, Lisa came out with the diamond. It felt like a heist, but no one was stealing anything.

She handed me a small, clear plastic case. It felt like holding a hundred newborn babies at the same time; I was very nervous. The case honestly looked like something you would win from the claw machine at an arcade. But sitting inside that cheap case on a little bed of foam was the diamond itself. I've never seen a diamond that big in real life—5.56 karats is like the spear end of an asparagus. I sat at my keyboard for ten minutes trying to think of what vegetable to compare it to, and that's what I came up with.

Lisa handed me an appraisal statement listing the value of this gemstone, which was much higher than the figure she had told me in the hotel lobby. The appraised value was actually $238,000. Lisa had said $150,000 because a diamond appraisal doesn't necessarily equal the real market value, so that's what she believed we could get for it when we sold it.

As Lisa was telling me these things in a public parking lot that seemingly felt less secure by the moment, she also assured me that if I lost the diamond, the insurance would cover it. I love Lisa, but I didn't quite trust her opinion on the insurance policy. After my speech in Vegas, I had to travel to New York City for another event before going home to Ohio. I was worried out of my mind.

From the minute Lisa dropped me off at the airport through my entire journey home, I was sweating bullets. That night, while I was at the airport waiting to board a plane for New York City, I felt like I was being watched the whole time. People would accidentally bump into me, and I would have a handful of micro panic attacks inside.

As I arrived in New York City, made my speech, and ultimately headed home to Cleveland, I kept thinking that I should check if the diamond was still in my bag. *But then*, I thought, *if I check the bag, while I'm checking it, what if it gets lost while I check it?*

I should check it.

I shouldn't check it.

I probably should.

Not check it.

I spent a lot of time staring at my bag and having an inner dialogue that sounded something like that.

I did eventually make it home safely with the diamond in hand, and now it is located in a secure bank.

What is the moral of the story? To be honest, I am not entirely sure, but we do have a huge diamond for sale, if you are looking for that sort of thing. It's huge and shiny. It would make a great gift. You can probably tell at this point that I'm not a good diamond salesman. They didn't teach me how to do this in college, but I'm trying. If you buy the diamond, all the proceeds will help our charitable programming, and I will give you a ten-minute hug. Actually, that sounds creepy now that I have written it out. Cancel the hug. Unless that's what you want. ■

Appraisal Certificate
For

Last Name _____   First Name _____   Date __11-18-14__

Address _____

City _____   State _____   zip __89102__

Current Markets: Gold __$1,150.00 OZ.__   Silver __N/A__   Platinum __N/A__

This is to certify that we have carefully examined the articles listed below and appraised those articles at current fair market replacement value. This certificate does not constitute an offer to purchase or replace articles.

Description	Appraised Value
LADIES PLATINUM AND DIAMOND RING	
ONE LADIES PLATINUM AND DIAMOND RING, WITH 161 ROUND,	
BRILLIANT CUT DIAMONDS, 8.96 CT.TW. THE CENTER DIAMOND	
IS 5.54 CT. ROUND, BRILLIANT CUT, SI1 CLARITY, E COLOR.	
G.I.A. CERTIFICATE REPORT #12569500; PRONG SET. THERE ARE	
2 EACH .71 CT. 1.42 CT.TW. BRILLIANT CUTS ON EACH SIDE OF	
THE CENTER, SI1 CLARITY, F COLOR, PRONG SET. THEY ARE	
SURROUNDED BY 158 ROUND, BRILLIANT CUT DIAMONDS, 2.0 CT.TW.	
SI1 CLARITY, F COLOR, BEAD SET.	
SEMI MOUNT, RETAIL VALUE=	$17,600.00
5.54 CT. RETAIL VALUE=	$235,000.00
TOTAL RETAIL VALUE=	$252,600.00

Appraised values are based upon our estimates of size and quality of the aforementioned articles. Appraiser assumes no responsibility to any action which may be taken with respect to this document.

Appraised By _____ MASTER JEWELER / OWNER

Appraiser's Signature _____ Date 1/8/201

Phone _____   www._____com

The Hallway of Third Grade

Dr. Hernandez Still Remembers

D r. Trisha Hernandez was a tenure track professor at California Baptist University in Riverside, California. At age twenty-eight, that's pretty legit.

While she was on a trip to Spain, Trish heard a *because I said I would* speech and was so moved that she decided to reach out to me directly to see if there was anything she could do as a volunteer for the cause back in the States. I had an event coming up in Los Angeles, about an hour away from where she lived, and asked if she could volunteer at one of our event tables afterward. At that table, we talked about how the organization was growing. Ultimately, Trish decided that she was going to apply for the only position open at our organization at the time: executive assistant to

the founder. Trish was willing to cut her salary in half and set aside her ten-plus years of education experience to calendar meetings. Why? Because of a single event that occurred when Trish was in the third grade.

She still remembers that particular moment in 1993 very clearly. It was the day of her school's art show, and Trish was in a classroom, looking around for her father. He was late, but she was still hopeful that he would show up. Eventually, Trish's dad walked in the room. He walked over to her and said that he loved her. Her dad then said that he would never see her again. Trish was told that her father was leaving the country after a divorce from her mother. For the rest of her life, she will never forget crying in the hallway at school.

Trisha Hernandez joined our team on July 8, 2015. Starting as my assistant, she helped me and *because I said I would* get through some pretty hard times. Trish was quickly promoted to become our vice president of character education. Today, she applies her experience, doctorate-level education, and skills to create personal development and service-learning programming for kids. Maybe she can reach another third grader out there who needs help understanding that they can be better than the people that break promises to them. ■

Never Means Never

The Responsibility of a Caregiver

Michelle Fishpaw was at a department store one day in Columbus, Ohio. Passing clothing racks, shoes, and accessories, she was stopped by a complete stranger.

"Are you Michelle Fishpaw?" the stranger asked.

"Yes," Michelle replied.

The woman then explained that back in 2000, both her family and Michelle's family were on the waiting list for the same babysitter. This woman gave up her spot on that list, which then made room for Michelle's daughter, Claire.

"You took our place . . . and I am so sorry," this stranger said.

In that moment, Michelle understood why this stranger felt the need to say something. That babysitter was convicted of a felony for what she did to Michelle's daughter in 2000.

Reflecting back on those events that occurred eighteen years ago, Michelle told me that "Mindy had all the right answers." Mindy was a babysitter who had come with strong recommendations from a local nonprofit that helps match families with childcare workers. These babysitters have to pass background checks *and* must provide at least three personal references. Mindy said that she had been a

Michelle and her daughter, Claire

nurse and had taught in Upper Arlington Schools, located in a charming suburb near where Michelle lived. Not only that, but Mindy also took care of the son of Michelle's neighbor, who was the anchor for a local television news station in Columbus.

Michelle remembers that waiting list very well and thought it was a spark of luck when a spot opened up for her first daughter. As a new mother, Michelle was wary of trusting anyone with caring for her baby as she returned to her teaching job. Michelle interviewed five other babysitters, but Mindy's impressive credentials were too good to pass up. In February 2000, Mindy began taking care of Claire, who was eleven months old at the time.

The incident that would change Claire's life forever happened only four days into her time with Mindy. It was three days before Claire's first birthday.

On Monday, February 28, 2000, Michelle went to pick up her daughter at the end of her teaching day at around 3:30 p.m. Michelle walked up to Mindy's house and rang the doorbell. She waited for the door to open for what seemed like an uncomfortable amount of time. When it eventually opened, Michelle heard crying immediately. Obviously, it is common for children to cry, especially at a stranger's house, but as Michelle later said, "This was a different kind of crying than I have never heard before." It sent chills down her spine.

Michelle wasn't certain which child it was, so she ran inside. Lying face down on the floor under a skylight was her daughter. Claire could barely lift her head. Michelle turned Claire over on to her back, expecting to see her daughter's bright blue eyes, but Claire's pupils were dilated to such an extreme that Michelle could not see color. Her eyes looked like black marbles.

At first, Michelle thought her daughter was having some sort of seizure. She wasn't sure what was going on, and with panic in her voice she said to Mindy, "Why didn't you call us? Have you called 911?" Mindy

wouldn't answer directly, and she seemed distant and strangely disconnected from the moment.

Michelle knew that she had to get her daughter to a doctor immediately.
She called their pediatrician's office, but they couldn't see Claire for five
hours. Her symptoms seemed to be growing worse, and Michelle instructed
Mindy to call 911. As Michelle waited for emergency services, it seemed
that Claire had lost consciousness; her breathing was shallow, and she vom-
ited white foam. It felt like an eternity for that ambulance to arrive.

With lights flashing, the ambulance eventually pulled up to the resi-
dence. By coincidence, one of the emergency responders was someone that
Michelle grew up with. Michelle told him everything she knew, but that
wasn't very much. Michelle climbed into the ambulance, and the emergency response professionals examined her baby. They confirmed that
Claire was unconscious, and they hooked her up to an electrocardiogram,
more commonly known as an EKG. This is a machine that checks for
problems with the electrical activity in the heart. They put an oxygen mask
on this little child, and they flipped on the sirens.

Michelle and Claire were taken to Nationwide Children's Hospital,
where a medical team began running scans on Claire. In a hospital room,
Michelle and her husband, Jon, were informed that Claire had a bilateral
subdural hematoma and retinal hemorrhaging, injuries consistent with the
condition that is commonly referred to as shaken baby syndrome.

Michelle remembers hearing that diagnosis for the first time and thinking, *Well, it must be something else. Clearly, there's been some mistake. Maybe
Claire fell off a table, and Mindy was too ashamed to admit her negligence.*

The doctor then said something that would immediately dispel that
speculation: "Your daughter's wounds are similar to those from falling out
of a two-story window." There was no mistake.

Shaken baby syndrome can more easily be understood as abusive head
trauma. Babies have weak neck muscles, so when a baby or young child
is shaken, their brain moves back and forth inside their skull. This causes
blood vessels to tear and blood to pool around the brain, resulting in irrep-
arable damage to the baby's development.

Claire stayed unconscious for almost twenty-four hours. While she was in the hospital, Clair was having up to fifteen seizures a day. The neurologist explained that these seizures were the body's reaction to having blood on the brain. Michelle slept at the hospital that night, refusing to leave her baby girl. She remembers waking up in a hospital room, feeling like she was literally waking from a nightmare, but then realizing that her surroundings were not those of her home. This was not a bad dream. This was real.

After Michelle woke up in the hospital on February 29, the day following the assault, she heard someone knock at the door and say softly, "Your little girl is waking up." Michelle got up and ran down the hallway to her daughter's room. The moment she came through the door still haunts her to this day.

"Claire was afraid of me. She didn't recognize who I was," Michelle says, recalling that day.

That is a look that no mother should have to see on the face of her own child. "All I wanted to do was help my baby," Michelle says. She felt helpless, wondering if her child was going to die, but everything was out of her hands.

In that hospital room, Michelle looked over at her husband, Jon, and at that moment, they made a promise to one another: If their child were to survive, they would make a difference so that this would not happen to other children.

Claire did survive. The damage to her frontal lobe resulted in impairments to her speech and movement; she takes daily medication to control seizures and migraines. As Claire grew up, she required an Individualized Education Plan because of the developmental needs that resulted from her abuse. Even so, it is clear that Claire's recovery from her injuries is quite miraculous. Her academic achievements have been recognized by the National Honor Society. She graduated Upper Arlington High School in 2017, earning four different scholarships.

It took a very long time, but eventually, Mindy was found guilty on two counts of child endangering. Over the course of eight years, Jon and

Michelle saw their promise to help other children like Claire as a commitment to advocacy. They attended many conferences about shaken baby syndrome. They spoke to medical professionals, emergency responders, and law enforcement professionals about the dangers of this form of child abuse. They met with other parents who had suffered through similar situations. Desperate to create awareness and prevention on a massive scale, Michelle and Jon advocated for legislative change around the issue of shaken baby syndrome.

On February 29, 2008, their promise was kept in the form of Ohio Revised Code 3701.63, collectively known as Claire's Law. This law mandates that educational materials must be distributed to expectant and new parents through hospitals, physicians' offices, childbirth educators, and all licensed childcare centers.

It can be hard for Michelle and Jon to talk about what happened, but imagine what it is like for Claire. Claire never wanted to be treated differently. But sometimes, kids at school can't understand that.

"Claire Gets Her Law,"
The Cincinnati Enquirer,
December 1, 2007.

As a part of *because I said I would*'s character education programming, I had the opportunity to give an assembly speech at Claire's middle school in Columbus when she was in the eighth grade. That day, Claire heard about our nonprofit for the first time, and by chance, she also received a free ticket to the inaugural *because I said I would* event in Columbus on September 6, 2014. Claire attended the conference and decided that she wanted to share her story. In a video booth at the event, she sat by her mother's side. With a written Promise Card in hand, Claire looked into the camera and stated her promise.

"I promise to share my story to help others. To not be afraid to show who I am as a person."

Michelle and her daughter, Claire

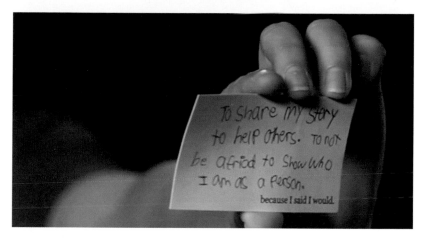

Claire then went on to advocate for shaken baby syndrome for the first time by making a public speech at a Rotary Club event in her area. She is now in her freshman year of college.

Ask any humanitarian how to help people, and somewhere in the conversation you have to talk about the law. It is not that we want to make everything political; it is just undeniable that legislation is a part of so many causes. Volunteer hours can do only so much. Even a donation of millions of dollars will eventually run out. Changing the law can make an impact on a massive and perpetual scale by mandating practices that can benefit generations to come. Michelle and Jon knew this would be the only way to reach parents across the country. ■

Hope

THE WORLD CAN GET BETTER

1. Self-Control
2. Compassion
3. Contemplation
4. Honesty
5. Accountability
6. Sacrifice
7. **Hope**

A promise needs hope to begin its life. For if it were not for hope, what would be the point of trying? Why should the alcoholic even begin to seek sobriety if they believe that sobriety is impossible? Why fundraise for a cure if you do not believe that one can be found? Hope is an essential part of what it takes to make a promise.

But too often we hope for miracles. We hope that a superhero will come along to solve it all. Unfortunately, we don't have enough time for miracles to show up, and superheroes don't exist. Sometimes what the world really needs is for people to just do what they said they are going to do in the first place. That's what I am hoping for.

Hope is like a road in the country; there was never a road, but when many people walk on it, the road comes into existence.

—LIN YUTANG

Being hopeful doesn't mean believing that everything will always be sunshine and roses. In fact, maybe the most hopeful people are those who actually believe the odds are gravely against them but who decide to try anyway. Saving a victim of human trafficking is not likely. Saving a kid from drowning is not likely. But sometimes the cost of success is living with the acceptance of failure. You place a bet and you hope.

Because I said I would has distributed millions of Promise Cards to people who have requested them from around the world. Is every card used? Is every promise kept? No. We send a hundred Promise Cards and hope for just a single change. Humanity has cured diseases, it has fought poverty, and it has ended wars. If there's a chance for all that, then there's a chance for us.

If the world feels dark and you do not see hope around you, that might be a sign that the hope is supposed to be you. *It's okay to think you can't do it, but that doesn't mean you're right.* ∎

CODE OF HONOR:

Hope

—

I believe that both I, and the world around me, can get better. I have hope and I wish to be what others have hoped for. I may not be around to see the impact of my promises, but I have faith that my actions were needed then and that they are needed now. I believe in the impact of a single individual. I have hope that others can believe the same.

- Use our character education materials, including lesson plans, videos, and other resources, in classrooms and youth development programs.

- Donate or raise funds to help support our charitable projects.

- Write a Promise Card to volunteer at another nonprofit near you and share it through social media.

- Invite a *because I said I would* speaker to share the importance of a promise at your organization's event.

Thank you for taking the time to read about *because I said I would* and the determination of our supporters. Since the day my father died, I have been fighting to ensure the survival of this cause, and being a part of this organization has been the honor of my life. In moments where I felt too weak to go on, nothing pulled me out of the ditch better than the promise stories that have been shared with us.

Please do not let our supporters' stories end as some sort of emotional entertainment. Colonel Parker Schenecker did not share the tragedy of his children to entertain anyone. Michelle Fishpaw did not relive Claire's abuse as a baby so that we could have a sad moment together. I don't talk about my father's death for your enjoyment. We share our stories for a single purpose: to encourage others to make and keep promises for the betterment of humanity. We are asking you to make a promise.

If there is any part of you that doesn't want this book to end, then it is time for you to become the next story. In this book you will find a Promise Card. I ask you to reach for it. Write down your commitment. Fulfill your promise. Others will see the adversity of your journey. When they ask you why you kept going when others would have quit, stare them right in the eye and say . . .

"because I said I would."

Acknowledgments

Thank you to everyone who helped make *because I said I would* a reality, especially Amanda Messer, Manish Patel, and our incredibly generous donors. Relating specifically to this book, I want to express a deep appreciation for all of our supporters who were willing to share their promise stories in these pages, to Julie Cartmill and Eric Unhold for helping to keep the book project organized, to the *because I said I would* staff for providing their perspectives, to Sally Collings for her support in writing and editing, to Paul Smith for helping me better understand storytelling, to Neil Gonzalez for his design expertise, and to Kimchi (my dog), who I am including in this section because she's a good girl.

About the Author

Alex Sheen is a four-time TEDx speaker and the founder of *because I said I would*, an international social movement and nonprofit dedicated to the betterment of humanity through promises made and kept. Sparked by a tragedy in his life, Alex created a concept called the Promise Card and began mailing them to anyone who requested one, at no cost to them. Since 2012, over 9.81 million Promise Cards have been distributed to over 153 countries.

Alex's unique perspective on accountability, commitment, and self-control developed from his responsibilities in leading a global effort about keeping promises, along with his personal experience in fulfilling his own promises. Alex once walked over 245 miles across the entire state of Ohio in 10 days, volunteered at 52 nonprofits in a single year, and has also ensured that 100 percent of his speaking engagement fees (over $1 million a year) go to charity.

Alex's work has been featured on *Good Morning America*, *The Steve Harvey Show*, the front page of Reddit, CNN, and many other programs. He is a very proud graduate of Ohio University, where he wants to give the commencement speech one day, but somehow Alex keeps getting beat out by other speakers. His plan now is to outlive all other famous people who have graduated from Ohio University. At that point, the president of the university will have no other choice but to choose him. Alex is also the kind of guy that starts to question if he should have asked someone else to write his own bio page. I mean, writing your own bio starts to feel pretty conceited, you know what I mean? But now it's too late to ask someone else because the publisher is hounding me to get this thing out the door. Plus, I have to go to this meeting in like 5 minutes and I don't have time for a redo.

Alex Sheen, he knows stuff.